A Chequered Life

Graham Warner and The Chequered Flag

Other great books from Veloce –

RAC handbooks
Caring for your car – How to maintain & service your car (Fry)
Caring for your car's bodywork and interior (Nixon)
Caring for your bicycle – How to maintain & repair your bicycle (Henshaw)
How your motorcycle works – Your guide to the components & systems of modern motorcycles (Henshaw)
Caring for your scooter – How to maintain & service your 49cc to 125cc twist & go scooter (Fry)
Efficient Driver's Handbook, The (Moss)
Electric Cars – The Future is Now! (Linde)
First aid for your car – Your expert guide to common problems & how to fix them (Collins)
How your car works (Linde)
Motorcycles – A first-time-buyer's guide (Henshaw)
Motorhomes – A first-time-buyer's guide (Fry)
Pass the MoT test! – How to check & prepare your car for the annual MoT test (Paxton)
Selling your car – How to make your car look great and how to sell it fast (Knight)
Simple fixes for your car – How to do small jobs for yourself and save money (Collins)

Those Were The Days ... Series
Alpine Trials & Rallies 1910-1973 (Pfundner)
Brighton National Speed Trials (Gardiner)
British and European Trucks of the 1970s (Peck)
British Drag Racing – The early years (Pettitt)
British Touring Car Racing (Collins)
Café Racer Phenomenon, The (Walker)
Drag Bike Racing in Britain – From the mid '60s to the mid '80s (Lee)
Endurance Racing at Silverstone in the 1970s & 1980s (Parker)
Hot Rod & Stock Car Racing in Britain in the 1980s (Neil)
Last Real Austins 1946-1959, The (Peck)
MG's Abingdon Factory (Moylan)
Motor Racing at Brands Hatch in the Seventies (Parker)
Motor Racing at Brands Hatch in the Eighties (Parker)
Motor Racing at Crystal Palace (Collins)
Motor Racing at Goodwood in the Sixties (Gardiner)
Motor Racing at Nassau in the 1950s & 1960s (O'Neil)
Motor Racing at Oulton Park in the 1960s (McFadyen)
Motor Racing at Oulton Park in the 1970s (McFadyen)
Motor Racing at Thruxton in the 1970s (Grant-Braham)
Motor Racing at Thruxton in the 1980s (Grant-Braham)
Superprix – The Story of Birmingham Motor Race (Page & Collins)

Rally Giants Series
Audi Quattro (Robson)
Austin Healey 100-6 & 3000 (Robson)
Fiat 131 Abarth (Robson)
Ford Escort MkI (Robson)
Ford Escort RS Cosworth & World Rally Car (Robson)
Ford Escort RS1800 (Robson)
Lancia Delta 4WD/Integrale (Robson)
Lancia Stratos (Robson)
Mini Cooper/Mini Cooper S (Robson)
Peugeot 205 T16 (Robson)
Saab 96 & V4 (Robson)
Subaru Impreza (Robson)
Toyota Celica GT4 (Robson)

Biographies
Amédée Gordini ... a true racing legend (Smith)
André Lefebvre, and the cars he created at Voisin and Citroën (Beck)
Cliff Allison, The Official Biography of – From the Fells to Ferrari (Gauld)
Edward Turner – The Man Behind the Motorcycles (Clew)
Jack Sears, The Official Biography of – Gentleman Jack (Gauld)
Jim Redman – 6 Times World Motorcycle Champion: The Autobiography (Redman)
John Chatham – 'Mr Big Healey' – The Official Biography (Burr)
The Lee Noble Story (Wilkins)
Pat Moss Carlsson Story, The – Harnessing Horsepower (Turner)
Tony Robinson – The biography of a race mechanic (Wagstaff)
Virgil Exner – Visioneer: The Official Biography of Virgil M Exner Designer Extraordinaire (Grist)

General
1½-litre GP Racing 1961-1965 (Whitelock)
AC Two-litre Saloons & Buckland Sportscars (Archibald)
Alfa Romeo 155/156/147 Competition Touring Cars (Collins)
Alfa Romeo Giulia Coupé GT & GTA (Tipler)
Alfa Romeo Montreal – The dream car that came true (Taylor)
Alfa Romeo Montreal – The Essential Companion (Taylor)
Alfa Tipo 33 (McDonough & Collins)
Alpine & Renault – The Development of the Revolutionary Turbo F1 Car 1968 to 1979 (Smith)
Alpine & Renault – The Sports Prototypes 1963 to 1969 (Smith)
Alpine & Renault – The Sports Prototypes 1973 to 1978 (Smith)
Anatomy of the Works Minis (Moylan)
Armstrong-Siddeley (Smith)
Autodrome (Collins & Ireland)
Autodrome 2 (Collins & Ireland)
Automotive A-Z, Lane's Dictionary of Automotive Terms (Lane)
Bahamas Speed Weeks, The (O'Neil)
Bentley Continental, Corniche and Azure (Bennett)
Bentley MkVI, Rolls-Royce Silver Wraith, Dawn & Cloud/Bentley R & S-Series (Nutland)
BMC Competitions Department Secrets (Turner, Chambers & Browning)
BMW 5-Series (Cranswick)
BMW Z-Cars (Taylor)
BMW Boxer Twins 1970-1995 Bible, The (Falloon)
BMW Custom Motorcycles – Choppers, Cruisers, Bobbers, Trikes & Quads (Cloesen)
BMW – The Power of M (Vivian)
Bonjour – Is this Italy? (Turner)
British at Indianapolis, The (Wagstaff)
British Cars, The Complete Catalogue of, 1895-1975 (Culshaw & Horrobin)
BRM – A Mechanic's Tale (Salmon)
BRM V16 (Ludvigsen)
Bugatti Type 40 (Price)
Bugatti 46/50 Updated Edition (Price & Arbey)
Bugatti T44 & T49 (Price & Arbey)
Bugatti 57 2nd Edition (Price)
Carrera Panamericana, La (Tipler)
Chrysler 300 – America's Most Powerful Car 2nd Edition (Ackerson)
Chrysler PT Cruiser (Ackerson)
Citroën DS (Bobbitt)
Classic British Car Electrical Systems (Astley)
Cobra – The Real Thing! (Legate)
Cortina – Ford's Bestseller (Robson)
Coventry Climax Racing Engines (Hammill)
Daily Mirror 1970 World Cup Rally 40, The (Robson)
Daimler SP250 New Edition (Long)
Datsun Fairlady Roadster to 280ZX – The Z-Car Story (Long)
Dino – The V6 Ferrari (Long)
Dodge Challenger & Plymouth Barracuda (Grist)
Dodge Charger – Enduring Thunder (Ackerson)
Dodge Dynamite! (Grist)
Drive on the Wild Side, A – 20 Extreme Driving Adventures From Around the World (Weaver)
Ducati 750 Bible, The (Falloon)
Ducati 750 SS 'round-case' 1974, The Book of the (Falloon)
Ducati 860, 900 and Mille Bible, The (Falloon)
Ducati Monster Bible, The (Falloon)
Fast Ladies – Female Racing Drivers 1888 to 1970 (Bouzanquet)
Fate of the Sleeping Beauties, The (op de Weegh/Hottendorff/op de Weegh)
Ferrari 288 GTO, The Book of the (Sackey)
Fiat & Abarth 124 Spider & Coupé (Tipler)
Fiat & Abarth 500 & 600 – 2nd Edition (Bobbitt)
Fiats, Great Small (Ward)
Ford Cleveland 335-Series V8 engine 1970 to 1982 – The Essential Source Book (Hammill)
Ford F100/F150 Pick-up 1948-1996 (Ackerson)
Ford GT – Then, and Now (Streather)
Ford GT40 (Legate)
Ford Thunderbird From 1954, The Book of the (Long)
Formula 5000 Motor Racing, Back then ... and back now (Lawson)
Forza Minardi! (Vigar)
Funky Mopeds (Skelton)
GT – The World's Best GT Cars 1953-73 (Dawson)
Hillclimbing & Sprinting – The Essential Manual (Short & Wilkinson)
Honda NSX (Long)
Intermeccanica – The Story of the Prancing Bull (McCredie & Reisner)
Italian Custom Motorcycles (Cloesen)
Jaguar, The Rise of (Price)
Jaguar XJ 220 – The Inside Story (Moreton)
Jaguar XJ-S, The Book of the (Long)
Karmann-Ghia Coupé & Convertible (Bobbitt)
Kawasaki Triples Bible, The (Walker)
Kris Meeke – Intercontinental Rally Challenge Champion (McBride)
Lamborghini Miura Bible, The (Sackey)
Lamborghini Urraco, The Book of the (Landsem)
Lambretta Bible, The (Davies)
Lancia 037 (Collins)
Lancia Delta HF Integrale (Blaettel & Wagner)
Land Rover Series III Reborn (Porter)
Land Rover, The Half-ton Military (Cook)
Laverda Twins & Triples Bible 1968-1986 (Falloon)
Lea-Francis Story, The (Price)
Le Mans Panoramic (Ireland)
Lexus Story, The (Long)
Lola – The Illustrated History (1957-1977) (Starkey)
Lola – All the Sports Racing & Single-seater Racing Cars 1978-1997 (Starkey)
Lola T70 – The Racing History & Individual Chassis Record – 4th Edition (Starkey)
Lotus 49 (Oliver)
Mazda MX-5/Miata 1.6 Enthusiast's Workshop Manual (Grainger & Shoemark)
Mazda MX-5/Miata 1.8 Enthusiast's Workshop Manual (Grainger & Shoemark)
Mazda MX-5 Miata: The Book of the World's Favourite Sportscar (Long)
Mazda MX-5 Miata Roadster (Long)
Maximum Mini (Booij)
Mercedes-Benz SL – W113-series 1963-1971 (Long)
Mercedes-Benz SL & SLC – 107-series 1971-1989 (Long)
MGA (Price Williams)
MGB & MGB GT– Expert Guide (Auto-doc Series) (Williams)
MGB Electrical Systems Updated & Revised Edition (Astley)
Mini Cooper – The Real Thing! (Tipler)
Mini Minor to Asia Minor (West)
Mitsubishi Lancer Evo, The Road Car & WRC Story (Long)
Montlhéry, The Story of the Paris Autodrome (Boddy)
Morgan Maverick (Lawrence)
Morris Minor, 60 Years on the Road (Newell)
Moto Guzzi Sport & Le Mans Bible, The (Falloon)
Motor Movies – The Posters! (Veysey)
Motor Racing – Reflections of a Lost Era (Carter)
Motor Racing – The Pursuit of Victory 1930-1962 (Carter)
Motor Racing – The Pursuit of Victory 1963-1972 (Wyatt/Sears)
Motorsport in colour, 1950s (Wainwright)
MV Agusta Fours, The book of the classic (Falloon)
Nissan 300ZX & 350Z – The Z-Car Story (Long)
Nissan GT-R Supercar: Born to race (Gorodji)
Northeast American Sports Car Races 1950-1959 (O'Neil)
Nothing Runs – Misadventures in the Classic, Collectable & Exotic Car Biz (Slutsky)
Off-Road Giants! (Volume 1) – Heroes of 1960s Motorcycle Sport (Westlake)
Off-Road Giants! (Volume 2) – Heroes of 1960s Motorcycle Sport (Westlake)
Pass the Theory and Practical Driving Tests (Gibson & Hoole)
Peking to Paris 2007 (Young)
Pontiac Firebird (Cranswick)
Porsche Boxster (Long)
Porsche 356 (2nd Edition) (Long)
Porsche 908 (Födisch, Neßhöver, Roßbach, Schwarz & Roßbach)
Porsche 911 Carrera – The Last of the Evolution (Corlett)
Porsche 911R, RS & RSR, 4th Edition (Starkey)
Porsche 911, The Book of the (Long)
Porsche 911SC 'Super Carrera' – The Essential Companion (Streather)
Porsche 914 & 914-6: The Definitive History of the Road & Competition Cars (Long)
Porsche 924 (Long)
Porsche 928 (Long)
Porsche 944 (Long)
Porsche 964, 993 & 996 Data Plate Code Breaker (Streather)
Porsche 993 'King Of Porsche' – The Essential Companion (Streather)
Porsche 996 'Supreme Porsche' – The Essential Companion (Streather)
Porsche Racing Cars – 1953 to 1975 (Long)
Porsche Racing Cars – 1976 to 2005 (Long)
Porsche – The Rally Story (Meredith)
Porsche: Three Generations of Genius (Meredith)
Preston Tucker & Others (Linde)
RAC Rally Action! (Gardiner)
Rallye Sport Fords: The Inside Story (Moreton)
Roads with a View – England's greatest views and how to find them by road (Corfield)
Roads With a View – Wales' greatest views and how to find them by road (Corfield)
Rolls-Royce Silver Shadow/Bentley T Series Corniche & Camargue – Revised & Enlarged Edition (Bobbitt)
Rolls-Royce Silver Spirit, Silver Spur & Bentley Mulsanne 2nd Edition (Bobbitt)
Runways & Racers (O'Neil)
RX-7 – Mazda's Rotary Engine Sportscar (Updated & Revised New Edition) (Long)
Singer Story: Cars, Commercial Vehicles, Bicycles & Motorcycle (Atkinson)
Sleeping Beauties USA – abandoned classic cars & trucks (Marek)
SM – Citroën's Maserati-engined Supercar (Long & Claverol)
Speedway – Auto racing's ghost tracks (Collins & Ireland)
Sprite Caravans, The Story of (Jenkinson)
Standard Motor Company, The Book of the
Subaru Impreza: The Road Car And WRC Story (Long)
Supercar, How to Build your own (Thompson)
Tales from the Toolbox (Oliver)
Toleman Story, The (Hilton)
Toyota Celica & Supra, The Book of Toyota's Sports Coupés (Long)
Toyota MR2 Coupés & Spyders (Long)
Triumph Speed Twin & Thunderbird Bible (Woolridge)
Triumph Tiger Cub Bible (Estall)
Triumph Trophy Bible (Woolridge)
Triumph TR6 (Kimberley)
TWR Story, The – Group A (Hughes & Scott)
Unraced (Collins)
Velocette Motorcycles – MSS to Thruxton – New Third Edition (Burris)
Volkswagens of the World (Glen)
VW Beetle Cabriolet – The full story of the convertible Beetle (Bobbitt)
VW Beetle – The Car of the 20th Century (Copping)
VW Golf: Five Generations of Fun (Copping & Cservenka)
VW – The Air-cooled Era (Copping)
Which Oil? – Choosing the right oils & greases for your antique, vintage, veteran, classic or collector car (Michell)
Works Minis, The Last (Purves & Brenchley)
Works Rally Mechanic (Moylan)

www.veloce.co.uk

First published in November 2013 by Veloce Publishing Limited, Veloce House, Parkway Farm Business Park, Middle Farm Way, Poundbury, Dorchester, Dorset, DT1 3AR, England. Fax 01305 250479/e-mail info@veloce.co.uk/web www.veloce.co.uk or www.velocebooks.com.

ISBN: 978-1-845844-13-4   UPC: 6-36847-04413-8

© Richard Heseltine and Veloce Publishing 2013. All rights reserved. With the exception of quoting brief passages for the purpose of review, no part of this publication may be recorded, reproduced or transmitted by any means, including photocopying, without the written permission of Veloce Publishing Ltd. Throughout this book logos, model names and designations, etc, have been used for the purposes of identification, illustration and decoration. Such names are the property of the trademark holder as this is not an official publication.
Readers with ideas for automotive books, or books on other transport or related hobby subjects, are invited to write to the editorial director of Veloce Publishing at the above address.
British Library Cataloguing in Publication Data – A catalogue record for this book is available from the British Library.
Typesetting, design and page make-up all by Veloce Publishing Ltd on Apple Mac. Printed in India by Replika Press.

A Chequered Life

Graham Warner and The Chequered Flag

VELOCE PUBLISHING
THE PUBLISHER OF FINE AUTOMOTIVE BOOKS

Contents

Introduction 6
Acknowledgements 7
Foreword by David Richards 8
Foreword by Ken Ellis 8
Foreword by Sir Jackie Stewart 9

I.   Learning to fly 11
II. The 'Flag is born 20
III. Onwards and upwards 31
IV. The stars align 42
V.   Supply and demand 53

VI.	Blazing trails	66
VII.	Lotus blossoms	79
VIII.	On a winning streak	91
IX.	Music, maestro, please!	107
X.	Rallying cry	117
XI.	Stealing the stage	130
XII.	The reckoning	142

Postscript 153
Index 159

Introduction

An awkward laugh tends to precede silence, not conversation. It's early 2011, and catching up with Graham Warner for the first time in almost a decade is freighted with trepidation. Rumour has it that he is still a mite peeved about something I wrote about him in an article for *Motor Sport* magazine several years earlier. Apparently, I'd labelled him "A name dropper." On coming face-to-face with him for the first time in ages he doesn't wait long to bring this up, the accused letting out a hollow laugh and mouthing silent objections. It isn't as though I had meant it *that* way. It's just that he knew a lot of people; a lot of well-known names in the motorsport world. Following the mother of all pregnant pauses, he breaks into a smile and asks: "How do you fancy working with me on a book?"

Graham was, and remains, a humble man. He is not one given to hype or eulogy. Indeed, it was quite a surprise to find ourselves collaborating on a biography, not least because he tends to shun the limelight and had hitherto been uninterested in discussing his motorsport career. However, over time he became increasingly keen to set a few records straight and explode a few myths – but first a few ground rules had to be laid down. If we were going to work together, the book had to be as much about the Chequered Flag team he created and those who raced for him as his own life. Nor did he want a chassis-by-chassis breakdown of each and every car he fielded, for one simple reason: that sort of thing bores him.

While writing this book, it soon became clear that Graham has been poorly served by history. As a racing driver, he excelled in sports cars. As an entrant, his team won in virtually every category it competed in, and as a bootstrap entrepreneur he went from selling cars from his driveway to running a string of marque agencies inside a decade. As a constructor, he took on the might of Cooper, Lotus, Lola, Elva, and countless other manufacturers in Formula Junior, and often beat them. And that's before you factor in his airborne exploits, or his spell as the owner of a record label, for that matter. Even in alleged retirement, he became a respected author and journalist specialising in aviation history, with several masterworks to his name.

But it was as a talent-spotter that he truly excelled. Graham's acute antennae for discerning ability in up-and-coming racing drivers in the late '50s and for much of the '60s was likely without equal. This is the man who gave the sainted Jim Clark his first ever race start in a single-seater; who also entered cars for everyone from Graham Hill to Mike Spence, Jackie Stewart to Jacky Ickx, before turning his attention to rallying. Typically, he chose only the best drivers to steer the most exotic cars on the national scene. The

'Flag was the only team to field a Lancia Stratos in the UK in period, achieving something the works squad never did: it made this mid-engined blunt instrument a winner on British soil. Rally fans of a certain age invariably get misty-eyed recalling the wailing Italian supercar in its black and white war paint, while perhaps being unaware that he actually ran *three* of these glorious machines over an eight year period.

However, as you will read, Graham's story isn't simply one of overachievement. There have been bad times, both personally and professionally. The business he founded and ran for close to 30 years was effectively swiped from under him; the Blenheim bomber he and his team spent ten years restoring was reduced to kindling shortly after completion. And producing this book wasn't without incident, Graham's life having been turned upside-down following the loss of his wife Shirley after 58 years of marriage. He also suffered a debilitating stroke shortly before the first words were committed to paper in 2012.

What I have learned from many hours spent in Graham's company is that he is nothing if not resilient. It isn't as though he's had a choice. But one thing is for sure, he has led a life less ordinary, and he has lived it well.

Richard Heseltine
London

Acknowledgements

This book wouldn't have been possible without the considerable assistance of the following: Formula Junior authority Nigel Russell for his endless patience and boundless knowledge of the subject, John 'Smudge' Smith for supplying the Blenheim restoration photos, and for providing valuable background info, Jim Dale and Bill Granger for their insider knowledge of the 'Flag's various racing programmes, and to team drivers Mike Walker, Roy Pike, Ian Ashley, Alec Poole, and Andy Dawson. So many people assisted this project so apologies to those whose names I have omitted to mention. You know who you are, and you have my undying gratitude.

All photos in this book are from the Graham Warner archive unless stated otherwise.

Forewords

Motorsport creates its fair share of extraordinary characters, but none more so than Graham Warner. With his roots so firmly established in motor racing, it was an extraordinarily bold move to venture into the world of rallying, and that is how I first came to know him.

As a Lancia Dealer via the Chequered Flag in Chiswick, Graham saw potential in the remarkable Lancia Stratos and set about building his own private rally team which, on many occasions, enjoyed giant-killing exploits, challenging the big factory teams of the time.

For me, it was a fantastic opportunity as a young co-driver to compete alongside the likes of Tony Pond, Billy Coleman, and Tom Pryce in the most iconic rally car of the era. For this, I will always be grateful to Graham.

There are thousands of fans out there who would never have had the opportunity of seeing a Lancia Stratos in action if it weren't for Graham Warner and his Chequered Flag rally team. It is on their behalf that I'd like to say a big thank you.

David Richards CBE
Founder and Chairman, Prodrive

There are plenty of petrol-heads that have managed the transition from wheels to wings; some are mentioned within these pages. None have made their mark in such an uplifting and determined manner as Graham Warner.

By his own admission, Graham was "An interloper," who "stumbled into the trials and tribulations" of historic aircraft. After a trip to Duxford in 1978 to see Robs Lamplough's nascent collection, he was left with a "... lasting concern" for a bundle of parts that could, in the right hands, become an airworthy Blenheim.

As a sprog aviation writer, I first got to know Graham in the early 1980s when I plucked up the courage to buttonhole him. He bowled me over when he announced that he "... devoured" editions of my book *Wrecks & Relics* to hunt out spare parts or new aircraft to join his British Aerial Museum. In late 1984 I became the editor of *FlyPast* magazine, and Graham was one of the first to congratulate me. Over the years he took on an unofficial role as my guardian angel, and I remember wincing as he berated my then boss over my "... ludicrous workload." I am not alone in having benefitted from Graham's sound advice and genuine concern.

Graham had a great team around him rebuilding

the Blenheim, but it needed a very special person to drive it forward, to keep spirits high, and when the answer was "No," to find new methods so that a "Yes" would be forthcoming. With great respect to the motor racing and rallying fraternity, you really have to be an aviator to know just how pioneering, complex and all-consuming the Blenheim project was. During this time, Graham earned a place in many hearts as a very special character; a gentleman with a warm sense of humour, unrelenting vision, and shedloads of perseverance.

Unknown to much of the aviation sector in 1984, Graham's 'other' world went through a seismic change. His beloved company, The Chequered Flag, was sold from underneath him and the Blenheim was on the books. Graham had to come to terms with the end of an era and the indignity of having to bid for what was effectively his own property. As the public got to know of the Blenheim, Graham felt the weight of expectation tumbling down on him from veterans, 'warbird' owners and operators, and enthusiasts. All eyes were on him and his crew.

On May 22 1987, a remarkably calm Graham called to say the first flight was about to happen. I hurtled down the M11 in Key Publishing's Ford Sierra (you can see how much of a petrol-head I am!), missed the sight of it in the air, but caught the euphoria of the team as those big, round engines ticked and cooled. Just 32 days later, we were on the phone again. In a moment of sheer stupidity, a senior airline pilot had ignored established procedures and carried out a touch-and-go during a display at Denham. The Blenheim was no more. Graham's stoicism was breathtaking; his main concern was that nobody was badly injured. As the weeks went by and the full meaning of the needless accident began to sink in, Graham would let slip bitter vehemence regarding the pilot's rashness. After all Graham had gone through, this venom was understandable and hopefully cathartic. Coming from such a mild and unflappable man, I found this glimpse of another side to him disturbing, but it wasn't long before his focus returned to that battered and abused bomber.

The team bounced back and decided to do it all again. Graham became an author to help raise funds, and his three books, *The Forgotten Bomber*, *Spirit of Britain First*, and *The Bristol Blenheim – A Complete History*, are enduring classics. There were difficult decisions to make regarding how the MkII rebuild could take place, and much of the British Aerial Museum fleet was sold.

The Blenheim took to the skies again on May 18 1993, becoming a much demanded and admired airshow star. Returning to Duxford in the summer of 2003, it encountered problems and was wrecked in a forced landing. There was no way Graham could fund the MkIII, and he was not prepared to go through the unending hoops of raising large sums. With a heavy heart his direct involvement with a world class and unique restoration was severed. Graham is still the revered figurehead of the Blenheim Society, the organisation that supports the bomber.

Graham has endeared himself to two very different, but closely linked, passions – high-performance cars and warbirds. Be it wheels, wings, or both, he has inspired countless people during his incredibly colourful, challenging, and chequered life.

Ken Ellis
Contributing Editor, *FlyPast*

In my opinion, Graham Warner has never been fully recognised for his contribution to British motorsport. In this book, there are a huge number of drivers from all around the world who have driven cars entered by Graham Warner and the Chequered Flag. Some of them went on to be giants in the world of motorsport, whether it be racing or even in rallying. To follow are just a few of the names that I have plucked out of a long list: Jim Clark, Graham Hill, Jacky Ickx, Geoff Duke, Frank Gardner, Peter Gethin, Tony Maggs, John Whitmore, Björn Waldegård and even JYS, plus a lot more! In fact, because of the success that the team enjoyed, it is sometimes forgotten that Graham Warner himself was extremely skilled behind the wheel.

I was very impressed and excited when Graham asked me to drive the Chequered Flag Lotus Elan against the cars driven by Jim Clark and Peter Arundel. Graham and his team gave an awful lot of drivers a real start in life; the chance to be recognised while racing against some of the best in the world. The development of a great many drivers was assisted by Graham and his team of very good mechanics. He was an entrant, he was a driver, and he was a sponsor – and a really big person in the world of high-performance car sales!

The swinging '60s and the trendy '70s were the eras which saw the Chequered Flag and Graham Warner at their very best. It was an exciting time for top-line drivers who would not only race a Formula One Car at an international motorsport event in Britain, but also GT cars, touring cars and sports cars, all on the same day.

Many people still feel that these were the halcyon days of British motorsport, when the young lions raced against – and sometimes even beat – the well-established giants of the sport. It was a time when versatility was part-and-parcel of a racing driver's curriculum: jumping from an F1 car, to a touring car, to a GT or a sports car. It provided a fantastic apprenticeship for people like me, and Graham Warner is one of those people who allowed me to be seen, along with so many others.

Graham is always effervescent; he is charismatic; for a driver to be considered good enough to drive for Graham Warner was a very big deal, and great feather in the cap. It's wonderful that Richard Heseltine has undertaken this book. He's been marvellous in his meticulous research, bringing back into focus the endeavours of a very special man during a very special window of time. Graham Warner created so much success and influenced so many people when the foundations of British motorsport were being newly laid for what has become one of the most important and successful contributors to Britain's prestige.

Congratulations Richard for the well-deserved but overdue recognition of one of Britain's major contributors; for the development of drivers and for the example shown by Graham Warner's commitment, drive, enthusiasm and success.

Sir Jackie Stewart OBE
Three-time Formula One Word Champion

I. Learning to fly

It was terrifying, exhausting and exhilarating by turn. Hunkered low in what passed for a passenger seat, Graham Arthur Warner savoured every moment: the joy of being in an expertly-guided racing car for the first time, the knot-in-the-stomach sensation of reaching unfathomable speeds, the penetrating sound of a supercharged straight-eight engine on open exhausts; the knowledge that life would never be the same again. Warner was barely out of his teens, but this voyage into the unknown would leave him a prisoner to his motorsport addiction. This giddying encounter was not just a revelation, it was affirmation – and this was after he had flown jet fighters in the Air Force.

The car in question was a prewar Bugatti Type 59, an object of beauty that, today, is fascinating to most people for its seven-figure value. In 1952 it was merely a recently obsolete Grand Prix racer that handily doubled as a road car. The driver was Rodney Clarke, owner of the famed Continental Cars dealership, and founder of the Connaught marque that would punch above its weight in Grand Prix and sports car racing that decade.

A passenger ride aboard Rodney Clarke's Bugatti Type 59 would have life-changing consequences for a young Graham Warner.

"My brother, Kennett, was a design draughtsman at Connaught, and one Sunday we were down at Continental Cars in Send, Surrey; me with my nose pressed against the glass outside the little showroom," Warner recalls. "There were all these exotic cars for sale but I was particularly taken by this beautiful Bugatti. It was pale blue, of course, with a rudimentary passenger seat and only the one aero-screen for the driver. Clarke appeared, and I enthusiastically asked him questions about the car. He then told me to hop in, handed me some RAF goggles, and off we shot down the Portsmouth Road at an almighty clip. And the noise! It went right through you. I also fell in love with the smell of Castrol R motor oil. There wasn't much in the way of traffic at that time, and Clarke wound up the Bugatti to 130mph along the A3. It was all quite safe, but the few cars we encounterd appeared to be almost stationary. I knew there and then that this was for me. I was going to be a racing driver."

There was, however, one rather obvious stumbling block. Warner wasn't born gagging on a silver spoon, but a lack of means would ultimately work in his favour over the long haul. He was nothing if not a self-starter. "Motorsport back then was very different to how it is now. There was no real sponsorship as such so unless you came from a wealthy background it was very hard to break into. But I looked around at the British stars of the day such as George Abecassis, Roy Salvadori, Reg Parnell, Tony Crook and Bob Gerard and realised that they were all in the motor trade. They sold cars during the week and raced at the weekend. I decided that this was obviously the right way to go, and that is why I eventually started the 'Flag."

Born May 31, 1929 to Charles Alexander Warner and Gladys Eve (née Wright), young Graham's sense of self-sufficiency and his interest in all things mechanical were apparent at an early age. "I was born in Lavender Hill, Battersea, in South West London. My father owned some drapers shops and we lived above one of them," he recalls. "My two elder brothers, Alexander and Kennett, were also born there. My father stood as a Conservative Party candidate for the borough council and later the county council, which resulted in the shop windows being smashed in, as Conservatives weren't overly popular in the area. I can still remember the broken glass covering everything. In 1934 the family moved to London Road in Twickenham, Middlesex, which wasn't far from the

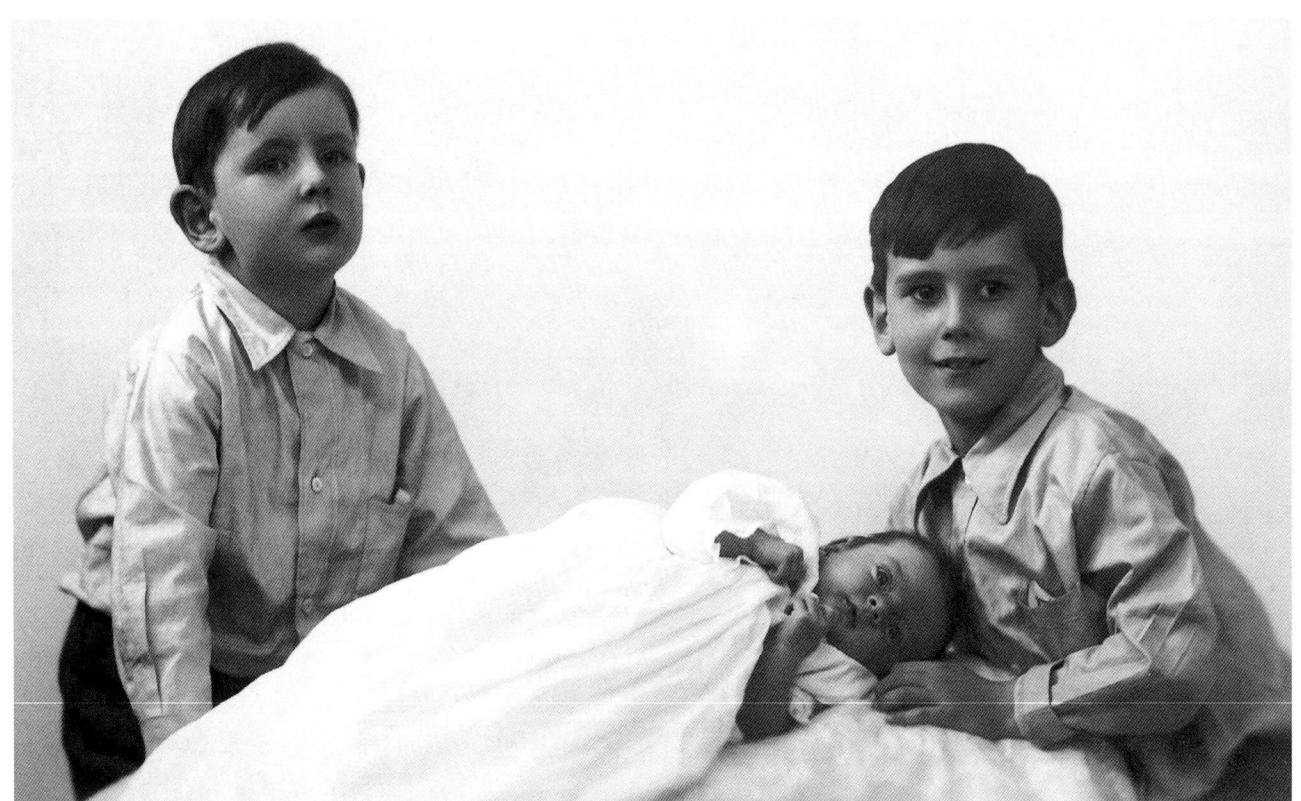

Baby Graham with his elder siblings Kennett (left) and Alexander.

Learning to fly

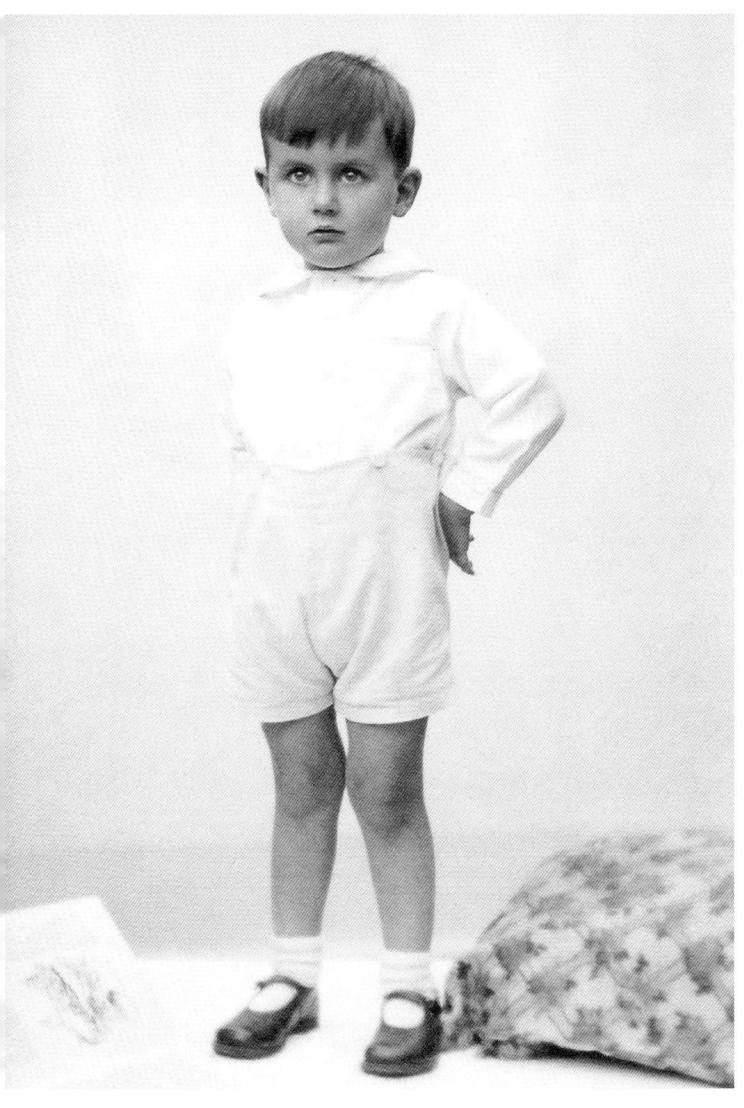

A cherubic Graham Arthur Warner, age five.

A love of music would be a constant theme throughout Warner's life. He is seen here as an innocent choirboy, aged 14.

famous rugby ground. Three years later we moved to a suburban semi in nearby Whitton, which is where I spent the war years.

"I went to the local Church of England school, but the big thing for me was joining the Whitton Cub Pack, and later the 11th Twickenham Scout Troop, which my brother Alex had founded – he was always keen on scouting. These days I think people massively underestimate the enormous influence the scouting movement once had on our youth. During World War II, around 80 to 90 per cent of air crews consisted of former scouts. Being a scout taught you leadership, initiative, and to always be prepared, which is an excellent motto. We did a lot of hikes out in the countryside, too, which were also massively beneficial in making you a more rounded individual. Being such a 'towny,' I hadn't even seen a cow until I was in the Scouts."

As Europe descended into hell at the end of the decade, Warner would experience loss of the gravest kind. "My oldest brother Alex joined the RAF when he was 17-and-a-half-years-old. He hadn't long finished his training when he was killed in action on April 21, 1943. This was shortly after his twentieth birthday."

The plane was returning to Pocklington, Yorkshire, following a successful bombing raid to Stettin, when it was hit by flak and crashed into the waters off Nyborg, Denmark. The captain and flight engineer survived and were picked up by boat to spend the rest of the war as prisoners. Tragically, bomb-aimer 1318828

A Chequered Life

The wartime family (L-R) – Alex Warner, Charles (father), Kennett, Eve (mother), and 10-year-old Graham in front. Warner Sr was too old for active service so served in the Army Pay Corps.

Alex Warner was killed, tragically, in action following a successful bombing raid to Stettin after his plane was hit by flak and crashed into the waters off Nyborg, Denmark.

Sgt Alex F Warner was among those who made the ultimate sacrifice. "I really looked up to him so it was a huge blow. Alex was a natural leader.

"Both of my brothers went to the Twickenham Technical College soon after it opened, and it was Kennett who fired my interest in the mechanical. I can clearly recall him taking me to places such as the Science Museum in London and showing me the sectioned engines. He would explain to me in detail how they worked; the differences between side-valves and overhead valves, or the advantages of overhead camshafts, and so on. I had all of that instilled in me from a very early age and it stuck. I was extremely fortunate in that regard."

A gifted student, Warner nonetheless batted away the notion of further education: a spell in academia was never on the cards. "The headmaster of Chiswick County Grammar School and the vicar of All Hallows Church on the Chertsey Road, where I was troop leader in the scouts, had spoken with those in authority at Magdalene College, Cambridge. One – or both – of them had gained their MA degrees there, and they were confident that I would be offered a place on an arts course. This was subject to me getting the right grades following my HSC (Higher School Certificate) exams, which you sat in the days before A-levels. They talked with reverence of 'Maudlin College' although I didn't fully comprehend what they were on about. I had no idea just how prestigious it was. But I was nuts on flying. That was what I wanted to do more than anything, so I only did one year in the sixth form and then joined the RAF the first moment I was able to. I never did sit my HSC exams. That upset just about everyone, not least my parents and my brothers. As for my headmaster …"

Unbowed, the defiantly self-directed 17-year-old left home in June 1947 and headed north to the Recruits Training Centre at RAF Padgate in Cheshire, before being dispatched to Shropshire a month later for a spell of abject misery. "Padgate was an awful place, but then we went to Bridgenorth for square-bashing which was infinitely worse. We had a particularly sadistic Junior NCO. Because we were air crew, we had white flashes on our hats to differentiate us. What that did in actuality was make us targets. Guys like him had sweated twenty years or more to become corporals and were full of resentment for us whippersnappers. They really put us through the wringer. In all honesty, it was bullying of the worst kind. We would be made to hold a rifle at high port – which is way above your head – for the most trivial

Warner, aged 16, as an ATC Cadet.

misdemeanour. Even if you hadn't committed one, they would make up something. They would stand an inch behind you, barking, 'Laddy, you need a haircut.' It was no use telling them you'd had one the day before. They would simply shout back, 'You need one when I say you need one.' It was the same with shaving. Your face could be as smooth as a baby's bum, but they would insist that it wasn't and put you on a charge. I hated every second of it."

Fast forward six months and Warner was faced with a dilemma. "I had the choice of two pilot courses – one based at RAF Spitalgate near Grantham, or another out in southern Rhodesia. I lied through my back teeth about how I had friends and family in Rhodesia, so instead of wet and windy Yorkshire I left the UK for sunny South Africa. I went out in December 1947 on an ancient troopship, the *Empire Trooper*, along with a load of army lads. It had been seized from the German navy during World War I, and by this point it was pretty ancient: it still had a vertical funnel and the smoke would often go ahead of you rather than stream behind you, depending on which way the wind was blowing. It took about a month to get out there, travelling via Gibraltar, Malta, Cyprus, Suez, Aden, Mombasa, and Durban. I then took a train to Bulawayo. I was based there for two years and got to see the whole of the African continent at the government's expense. It was a wonderful experience."

April 2, 1948 marked a personal milestone as Warner made his first solo flight, taking off from RAF Heaney, Bulawayo aboard a de Havilland Tiger Moth. "They were still plugging away and were used for elementary flying. It was a very simple aircraft – no brakes or flaps, and you had to swing the prop to start the engine – but it meant you had the most delightful fresh-air flying. It was also perfect for learning how to do proper three-point landings. From there we moved on to the Harvard, which was a good trainer. I received my 'Wings' on January 7, 1949 and returned to England in August of that year. I then continued my training with a bad weather flying course in South Cerney, Gloucestershire. For fairly obvious reasons that hadn't been on the curriculum back in Bulawayo. There was one runway and maybe three roads and a lake: night navigation was made that much easier because you could see for about 20 to 30 miles in the dark without any difficulty, and it didn't rain.

Warner in civvies on a Harvard T6 at RAF Heaney.

"That wasn't the case in the Cotswolds. We had a different model of Harvard and were made to do something called Beam Approach, which was an audible but not visual system intended to place the aircraft at the right height and speed on final approach to a runway obscured by mist, cloud or darkness. It should have been called Aural Torture. A transmitter at the runway threshold sent out Morse 'A's (dot-dash) and 'N's (dash-dot) about 2.5 degrees either side of the centre line, so you heard one if you were to the left or right of the centre, but of course you were flying down an ever-decreasing narrow V of constant noise, reducing height and speed, so even if you were on the correct heading you would fly out of one side or the other of the narrowing beam. There was an outer marker of slow, low-pitched notes and an inner marker of rapid, high-pitched notes that were superimposed on the noises of the beam, and you had to be at a certain height and speed over each. Add in the hisses and interference you would pick up on the radios of that period – the Harvard being an extremely noisy aircraft anyway – and it really was aural torture.

"On top of all that, we had yellow screens over the windows and wore blue goggles to ensure that we couldn't see out of the cockpit, the idea being that you had to rely on the instruments and your senses. When the instructor said 'remove goggles,' if you were lucky the end of the runway was disappearing under the aircraft's nose and you were clear of land. An hour of this cacophony led to ringing in the ears and a splitting headache. It was an incredibly difficult thing to do correctly, but you had to keep doing it until you got it absolutely right. Once I had completed the bad weather training, I then joined a night fighter squadron flying Mosquitos out of Brize Norton, but it was subsequently disbanded and I was sent on indefinite leave – which isn't great when you need to be flying constantly."

In late 1949, while awaiting a vacancy on the Mosquito OTU, Warner was attached to 149 Squadron Bomber Command at Mildenhall, Suffolk, as a second pilot. "They operated Avro Lincolns, a larger development of the Lancaster, and I was attached in order to give me some flying practice time. The Lincoln seemed enormous after the Tiger Moths and Harvards I had flown up to then. We did night-fighter affiliation exercises with Fighter Commander Mosquitos, where they attempted to intercept us using radar. We also performed 'Bullseye,' a night bombing exercise to the Heligoland islands."

Such manoeuvres wouldn't be without incident,

Warner immediately after the Wings parade at RAF Heaney in 1950.

some of them intentional. "It was while on one of these exercises that a young Pilot Officer Captain had some difficulties with a rather boisterous crew of Aussies and Canadians. They threw their clip-on parachutes in a pile by the entrance door in the rear fuselage rather than place them in the proper stowage position by each crew station as he had asked. Only the pilots' parachutes were strapped on, and we sat on them in specially shaped seats. The other crewmembers wore a harness with chest clips to attach the 'chutes should they be needed.

A Chequered Life

"We had been flying for quite a few hours, the engines droning away. Most of the crew had dozed off or were reading or playing cards, when the skipper said, 'Watch this.' He suddenly throttled back all four engines. The result was instant silence, which was livened shortly thereafter by spectacular pops and bangs and flames from the open exhausts – from 48-cylinders – with the aircraft then dropping several hundred feet. It really startled me, and I could actually see what was happening! He then got on the intercom and said, 'Stand by to abandon aircraft,' and pandemonium broke out as six crewmen tried to find their 'chutes in the back of the aircraft. This was a very difficult thing to do in such a confined space, and arguments inevitably flared up. The skipper had made his point (somewhat graphically), and cancelled his order, saying: 'Perhaps now you will stow your 'chutes properly.' After that, they did."

In the space of two years, Warner had gone from practicing aboard a basic biplane to joining the Jet Age, and had experienced massive evolutionary leaps in aviation design. "In April 1950 I was with the Advanced Flying School, flying Meteors from RAF Driffield in Yorkshire for three months before returning to the south of England to the Operational Conversation Unit flying Vampires from RAF Stradishall in Suffolk. The Vampire was quite simple to fly, but it had a few nasty tricks. It would flick out of a turn if you loaded it with too much G-force, which was very dangerous at low level. Of course it was a subsonic aircraft, so if you approached its limiting Mach number it would porpoise badly and start to shake itself to bits. The Meteor had some vices, too. If you extended the air brakes to slow it to the limiting speed for lowering the wheels, you had to retract the air brakes before selecting 'wheels down,' or the combination would so disrupt the airflow over the tail surfaces that control could easily be lost. The early jet engines would flame out if the throttles were opened too quickly which made close formation flying quite tricky – and don't forget we didn't have ejector seats. I flew only single-seat Vampires prior to the introduction of the two-seater T11 Trainer version. A great number of both types were lost through accidents – usually fatal ones – for those were pioneering days."

1951 would prove a pivotal year for Warner. Having earned his spurs in a variety of aircraft, he decided that life in the armed forces wasn't for him. "I developed a hernia after hand-cranking a car, and had to come off flying duties for an operation. While I was recuperating, I took the opportunity to leave the

RAF. I loved the flying side but by that point I was fed up with all the 'bull' and red tape that came with it."

Without a job in 'Civvy Street' awaiting him, Warner embarked on life as a car dealer, just like his motor racing idols. In order to do this, first he had to buy a car of his own. "My first was a Riley Nine 'special,' registration number MY5481. It was essentially a cut 'n' shut saloon car with a rather rudimentary, doorless two-seater body made of aluminium. It had cycle-type wings, wire wheels, a fold-flat windscreen, an alloy gear change extension with a tiny gearlever (possibly

Warner was an early member of the jet set, seen here piloting a Meteor IV in 1950.

from a Riley Imp), and it was rather a racy looking thing. It went quite well, too; even more so after I added four Amal carburettors, a high compression cylinder head and a four-branch Servais exhaust system.

"I greatly enjoyed driving it to events. I went down to circuits such as Goodwood and Silverstone where I got to see the great Froilán González, 'The Pampas Bull,' win the 1951 British Grand Prix for what was Ferrari's first ever victory in a World Championship Formula One race. He defeated the hitherto dominant works Alfa Romeos in the process, and was great to watch. This only reinforced the desire to compete myself. I did a couple of driving tests in the Riley which were quite popular at the time."

However, the leap from aspiring racing driver to circuit star would have to wait a while longer.

II. The 'Flag is born

Having traded in his flight suit for business attire, Graham Warner embarked on his new life as a motor trader following a well-trodden path: initially, he sold cars from home. Armed with a gratuity of £200 on leaving the RAF, and full of ambition, he was about to inch his way closer to his motorsport dream, one deal at a time. "My father had died in 1949 while I was out in Rhodesia. Midway through 1951, my mother decided to sell the house in Whitton and move to Canada, where she had relatives. She would return a year later, but by this time my brother, Kennett, and I were living in a nice first floor apartment on Gunnersbury Avenue overlooking Ealing Common, from where we dealt in sports cars. The apartment was within a lovely Victorian house with what had been a coach house at the foot of the garden, which had been turned into a four-car garage. It also had a large concrete forecourt with off-road parking for another four cars. In many ways it was perfect."

Having a clientele already in place also helped to ease the transition. "Friends in the Air Force would look at my car and say, 'that's nice, can you get me one?' so I would go out and find something similar. Kennett and I would also work on the cars at home; do engine overhauls and that sort of thing."

There were, however, a few wrinkles in the business plan. "Fixing cars, or having stock on the driveway, didn't sit well with some of our neighbours who complained to Ealing Council. It came down from on high that there could be no 'trading activity in a residential area,' and that was that. We were effectively banned, so I took a job as a junior salesman at Performance Cars on the Great West Road in Brentford, Middlesex, while Kennett joined Connaught as a designer/draughtsman.

"For me it was fascinating to be close to that level of racing, even if it was on the periphery via my brother. There used to be an experimental department (a shed, really) at the back of the Connaught works in Ripley where they would run an engine on a brake. They had a high-speed camera set up so they could film the valve gear working. They could then slow the film, see the cams hit the follower and shoot up the pushrod and on to the cam. The valve would then hit and detach from its spring for a split second. It was a remarkable thing to watch."

His own competition career, however, was still stuck in neutral. "At that point, Kennett owned the very special ex-Paul Pycroft Jaguar which had been heavily reworked for racing."

This machine, a prewar SS100 clothed with a bespoke streamlined body, had the distinction of winning the first ever race at Goodwood on September

The 'Flag is born

Cisitalia 202MM was just one of many exotic and unusual sports cars to be sold by Graham and Kennett Warner while trading from their home overlooking Ealing Common.

Warner's competition career began aboard this ex-Richard Stallebrass Aston Martin 2-litre Speed model.

Warner attends to the Kieft-Ford at Castle Combe, 1953. His race debut would have to wait a little longer after a front upright failed in practice.

18, 1948. "It was a remarkable-looking thing, and there were rumours that it had inspired the styling of the Jaguar XK120 production car, but that may be apocryphal. [Kennett] buying that car spurred me on, as I decided I needed something quicker!"

Warner found just the ticket in the form of a prewar ex-Richard Stallebrass Aston Martin. "It was a 2-litre Speed Model with an Ulster body and was registered JAB8. It was the sister car to the one in which St John Horsfall won the '46 Belgian Grand Prix at Spa Francorchamps. It was a great car and went like a rocket. I did a few driving tests in it and had a run at Shelsley Walsh. Those were the days when you would go haring up the hillclimb wearing a beret rather than a crash hat. It was huge fun, and to be in your early twenties and own a car like that was rather special."

It was joined by a purpose-built racer, of a sort, shortly thereafter. "I bought a Kieft which at one point had been a rear-engined, motorcycle-powered Formula Three car. By the time I got the car it had a souped-up Ford sidevalve engine in the front and a ghastly, angular body. It looked awful, but it was superb to drive. When I bought the car, it was fitted with a set of Michelin Wire Sole tyres, with a coil of wire embedded in the tread. As the tyres wore down, the ends of each coil became exposed, so if you cornered hard enough you would get a lovely shower of sparks. This was very good on a dark night! I entered it for my first ever race at Castle Combe in 1953, and put up some good times in practice, but a stub axle broke so I couldn't participate in the actual race."

The long-awaited circuit debut would have to wait a while longer, as there were one or two other distractions that curtailed his competition activities. "I met Shirley Newby Kenyon in 1952. She was a tall, slim 19-year-old trainee beautician living in digs in Ealing. The Dome filling station on the Great West Road just up from Performance Cars had a small coffee bar, and I used to see her there. She was keen on cars and had noticed that I usually turned up in a different one each time. I finally persuaded her to go for a spin with me in a Lagonda VdP Tourer. On July 20, 1954 we were married at Iver Parish Church in Buckinghamshire."

On a professional level, Warner was soaking up experience in the motor trade. "I learned a lot at Performance Cars, mostly what not to do. I was the only one there who could write properly, so I did all the correspondence, advertising, and admin. It was an interesting place to work, if that is the right word, and I came into contact with some colourful characters. You have to remember that the motor trade in the 1950s wasn't as regulated as it is now, and there were a few rogues out there who were involved in things they shouldn't have been. One particular episode that

Warner married Shirley Newby Kenyon in July 1954, and they were together for 58 years.

sticks in the mind involved a bullion robbery in the Piccadilly underpass. One evening a couple of vans turned up at Performance Cars. Some burly men got out and rather hurriedly carried things into the office that were clearly very heavy. These items were then put into the safe. Someone told me that these 'things' were actually 13 gold ingots. A couple of days later the law appeared, the safe was opened, and the boss was arrested. His defence was that he had been looking after them for a friend. How was he to know that they were stolen? At some point during the arrest and seizure, one of the ingots went missing …

"It was certainly an experience, that's for sure. It wasn't all bad, though. I got to drive some great kit, usually up the Great West Road after the boss had left. I went out in a lovely prewar straight-eight Maserati 26M, an ERA Grand Prix car, Frazer Nash Le Mans Rep; all sorts of things. The locals were used to it. I was pretty confident that I knew the business, and my time at Performance Cars reinforced my belief about how a business should be run – basically the exact opposite way to what I'd witnessed there! Anyway, in 1955 I became the manager of Carr Bros Garages' new sports car department in Purley, Surrey. I was given completely free reign, and was able to set up and run the whole thing as I saw fit. I was in charge of buying, selling and locating cars. It was very successful, too, and while I was only there for a year, it taught me that I could do it. It gave me the confidence to know that I could strike out on my own. Unfortunately, I was knocked for six that same year after my appendix burst. I developed Peritonitis – which is usually fatal – while I was in hospital, so it was a somewhat scary time."

After being laid low for two months, a recuperated and re-energised Warner followed through and

A Chequered Life

The Chequered Flag showrooms became a Mecca for sports car enthusiasts.

The 'Flag is born

became his own boss. "I'd seen this small showroom on the Fulham Road in South West London which had an office in the basement and room for maybe six cars in the showroom. In early 1956 I took a deep breath, signed my life away, and took on a short lease – and so the Chequered Flag was born. I thought long and hard about naming the business; about coming up with something appropriate. I didn't want to go down the clichéd route of Graham Warner Motors or suchlike. I was adamant from the beginning that I was only going to deal in sports or sporting cars. I didn't want to sell estate cars or small saloons or whatever, as they didn't interest me. I wanted a name that sold the brand; something with strong motorsport connotations. I seem to remember toying with Pit & Paddock, but the Chequered Flag seemed perfect.

"The lease expired in December of that year and I had the option of renewing it or moving to somewhere larger. I had seen a big, empty showroom on Chiswick High Road which had formerly been a BMW motorcycle dealership and it seemed just the thing. Having said that, there was cause for concern. We had done well that summer but this was smack bang in the middle of the Suez Crisis which had crippled the supply of petrol to British pumps. This obviously had a knock-on effect on the sports car market, so there was a degree of internal discussion ... should I, shouldn't I? I then put my head on the block and took out a ten-year lease. Fortunately, I got it right, as 1957 proved to be an absolutely stunning year for us. Our moving into the new and much, *much* larger premises coincided with a boom in domestic purchasing: cars, furniture, television sets, radios, and so on. We sold more than 1000 cars that year, which was truly remarkable. Before long we had a buying department with two or three people perpetually scouring the country for good sports cars. Unfortunately, one of my best buyers then creamed off the best cars and went off on his own, but overall it was a brilliant time.

"I was resolute in what the 'Flag was going to represent and how we should deal with our customers. I wanted only enthusiasts on the sales team. I hated that whole sheepskin and trilby stereotype that was part and parcel with the motor trade in those days. In 1957 I would have been 28-years-old, and I don't think there was a salesman who worked for me who was older than 25 years of age. I wanted to go racing, and so did the staff. I was always careful in hiring the right people. If I interviewed anyone for a job as a sales assistant, I was mainly concerned with how much they knew about cars and how keen they were.

I imposed on them to be honest, upfront and fair. I used to drill into them not to exaggerate – certainly not to lie. Describe what you are selling accurately and there will be no repercussions down the road. Obviously, we had to move cars on, and there were techniques. I can remember one chap coming into the showroom and umming and ahing over a car. His wife didn't want him to have it, so our salesman said, 'We'll see who wears the trousers in this household.' That was enough to clinch it. He bought the car and they left bickering!"

In January 1958, Martyn Watkins of *Autosport* magazine wrote breathlessly of the 'Flag: "Every day four or five cars are dealt with. All are sports or sporting types. Frazer Nash, HWM-Jaguar, Maserati, Emeryson, Lester, Lotus, Healey, Austin-Healey, MG, TR, Jaguar, Morgan, Aston Martin – they've had 'em all … Another feature of which the business is proud is the matter of after sales service: all cars less than five year old are covered by a three months guarantee while the buyer of an older vehicle can be sure of help and assistance. The firm, too, will help customers with spares problems while, naturally, every car offered for sale undergoes a thorough check on the road and in the workshops. In the latter department there are qualified trimmers, panel-beaters and fully experienced mechanics to leave little margin for dissatisfaction."

Watkins went on to add: "Pride of the stock when *Autosport* visited the firm was a 1.75-litre supercharged Alfa Romeo with Zagato bodywork and behind the car's presence lies a tale. The clue lies in its Italian registration plates, for when the firm acquired the car it was, in fact, snug at home in sunny Italy. So the car was duly brought to Chiswick – not by rail, but by road and under its own steam! And that is the sort of thing that seems to fill the atmosphere at The Chequered Flag: enthusiasm, efficiency and success. There, then, are the ingredients of a firm that, in 18 months, has reached the top. And it is indeed the top: at the end of the first financial year, the turnover had exceeded half-a-million pounds – and they're not finished yet!"

As the 'Flag rocketed into the public eye, Warner finally realised his ambition of going motor racing, but typically his competition programme was far from conventional. "I decided that in 1958 we as a business would get involved in motorsport with drivers from the sales team, which of course went down very well! My thinking was this: we would get publicity for the business, the troops would be happy, but they would also learn more about the cars. This would then help them in their jobs. Initially, the idea was to get involved in speed events – enter a few hillclimbs and sprints to get some experience – and then do some club races later on. We would also get training on the circuits from experienced drivers, Jack Fairman – who to be honest I didn't have much time for – and Percy Crabb."

The embryonic Chequered Flag Stable team consisted of an aluminium-bodied Austin-Healey 100S, one of just 55 made, and an ex-Keith Hall first-series Lotus Eleven-Climax. "We wanted to compete in the same type of cars that we sold, and initially we took cars from stock," Warner explains.

The driver line-up consisted of Warner, Alan Foster, David Briggs, Brian Wilkinson, Dennis St John and John Anstead, who would go on to become a co-concessionaire for Abarth in the UK. The équipe made its debut at the Surrey Sporting Motor Club's sprint at Brands Hatch for the season opener on March 2. The Kent venue would become a second home that year. Armed with the 100S, Warner ended the day second in the 3-litre class with Briggs, the firm's buying manager, spinning the Lotus out of the race at Clearways, this being the first time he had so much as driven the car. At the same meeting, Warner borrowed a hardtop for the Healey and entered it for PR man John Webb, at Webb's suggestion, in the closed car class, which he duly claimed.

Webb, whose name would in time become inextricably linked with Brands Hatch in his longstanding role as circuit manager, was on a retainer with Warner, although their relationship would in time become strained. "He was a very good publicist, and the 'Flag became well known in the national dailies thanks in part to him. Whenever we won, or crashed, it was always in the newspapers ... but I must admit I soon got tired of the whole 'jet pilot goes motor racing' angle most of the stories had. We fell out later on which was unfortunate, but he certainly aided our cause in the early years."

Returning to Brands Hatch later that same month for the Tunbridge Wells Motor Club Sprint, Warner recorded the fastest time in the Healey, only to have his final run curtailed by a broken stub axle as he entered the bottom straight. Another Lotus Eleven, this time an 1172cc Ford sidevalve-engined Club variant, had been purchased the evening before the meeting and was driven to class honours by Briggs. It represented the maiden victory for the fledgling squad – the first of many. St John, meanwhile, followed through a month later in a 250 Motor Racing Club sprint at Stapleford, driving the smaller-engined Lotus to claim 1200cc honours, with Anstead placing second. Suitably emboldened, Warner then sold the older Series I Eleven and replaced it with a new Series II Climax-powered car. "It had a de Dion rear end, disc brakes, magnesium wheels – the lot. As for it being brand new, well, we had to practically rebuild it. One of the wishbones had been installed upside down – all sort of things were wrong with it.

"At that same time I also added another car to the line-up; a Tojeiro-Bristol with a six-port 'head and lots of special parts. It was a lovely-looking car and had driven very well in Percy Crabb's hands. Like all of our cars back then, we re-did it in our black and white colour scheme, and then decided to enter Percy for the BRSCC Easter Monday meeting at Brands Hatch. I was too inexperienced to race something as hairy as that, and Percy knew the car well, so it made sense."

The result was fifth place in the Formula Libre race, Crabb having led for much of the way. That same meeting on April 7 1958 also marked Warner's debut in a motor race Armed with the proven Healey, he enjoyed a ding-dong battle with DJ Hayles' MGA in the 15-lap Series Production Sports Car event before placing second overall behind Bill Wilks' Frazer Nash Le Mans Replica. In the Warner-sponsored Chequered Flag Trophy race for 1100cc sports cars, Alan Foster finished sixth in the new, badly behaving, Lotus.

Sometime Grand Prix driver Jack Fairman was initially employed as a racer/driving coach. Here he gives instruction to 21-year-old 'Flag advertising assistant Valerie Johnson at Brands Hatch.

Percy Crabb finished fifth in the Formula Libre race at Brands Hatch in April 1958, having led for much of the way.

Returning to Brands Hatch on April 20, Percy steered the Tojeiro to second place behind John Bekaert's HWM-Jaguar in the Above 1200cc race while Warner drove the Healey to fifth in the seven-lap *Autosport*-backed production sports car contest. He had been running second for much of the way only to spin at Clearways. Then it all started to get very – *very* – expensive. After withdrawing from a meeting at Gosport following the death of a fellow competitor, the Chequered Flag Stable descended on Brands Hatch en-masse in early May for a Mid-Surrey Automobile Club sprint and high-speed trial. Warner, Percy and St John claimed class prizes aboard the Healey, Tojeiro and Lotus-Ford respectively, only for the latter to undo all his good work in the speed trial aboard the Lotus-Climax. Warner recalls: "Dennis spun at Clearways and the car struck a marshals' hut made of concrete, which was just about the only immovable object out there. There were a lot of accidents and blow ups that season, due largely to our lack of experience. The Lotuses in particular cost a fortune to repair. They had all-aluminium bodies made by Williams & Pritchard down in Edmonton, and we were forever getting Charlie Williams to make us new nose and tail sections. The bills really began to stack up."

Over the course of the season, the road-legal racers were generally driven to and from meetings. When an ex-Aston Martin transporter was acquired midway through the year, this prewar AEC coach-based monster often failed to cover itself in glory. Trainee administrator Mike Beuttler wrote in *Autosport*: "[It] showed a marked dislike to motor racing and it burst tyres spectacularly at the rate of one every time it was used. Then the gearlever broke and the vehicle became very unpopular and was not driven much after that!"

With Warner away in Monaco, Crabb was entrusted with the Healey for yet another run at Brands on May 18. He enjoyed a stirring battle with Ian Walker's

Warner made his circuit debut during the BRSCC Easter Monday meeting at Brands Hatch. He finished second in the ProdSports race aboard an ally-bodied Austin-Healey 100S.

Lotus Elite, and led for much of the race, only to retire the overheating roadster in the closing stages. It subsequently transpired that someone had forgotten to reattach the radiator cap after a post-practice top-up. A week later, a class win with the Healey at Stapleford preceded a maiden outing at Goodwood for the Whit Monday meeting. This resulted in further expense. Percy led the *Autosport*-backed production sports car race in the 100S, only to drop down to an eventual fourth with ignition trouble. Later that day, he was fortunate to emerge from a high-speed accident aboard the Tojeiro. Approaching Woodcote, he discovered a steering arm had broken and became a passenger.

It would only get worse. On June 8, the Healey dropped a valve during the *Autosport* production sports car race at Brands while leading Dick Protheroe's similar car. In the same race, Foster spun the team's Lotus-Climax entering the bottom straight and clouting the bank repeatedly – mercifully, without injuring himself. The repaired Tojeiro was subsequently moved on as Warner found it an expensive car to maintain, even before the many accidents. Besides, it was no longer competitive. Warner explains: "It got to the point where there were fewer and fewer places to race it. It was still quick in the 2-litre class of sports car racing, but that was dying off, which left Formula Libre where it was up against single-seaters and somewhat outclassed. I decided to replace it with a Lotus Seven which, to be honest, was anything but: it was essentially a Lotus 12 Formula Two car with a Seven body. She had been built at considerable cost, but the chap who had commissioned it overturned the car so it went back to Lotus to be rebuilt with a new chassis. Mike Costin did all of this and then advised the disillusioned owner that we should buy it off him. It was a super little car with a single-cam 1.5-litre Coventry Climax FWB engine, de Dion rear end, inboard disc brakes from the Lotus Eleven and 'Wobbly Web' magnesium wheels."

Once in 'Flag colours, Warner christened it with a sprint class victory at Brands on June 15, guest driver Jean Bloxham finishing second overall and taking the ladies' award while she was at it.

The Seven would serve the team admirably that season, largely because few team cars were in running order at any one time. The venerable Ford sidevalve-powered Lotus Eleven was comprehensively damaged during mid-week testing at Brands in June '58: company secretary St John missed a gear on entry into Paddock bend, stamped on the brake pedal and left the circuit, demolishing a wooden barricade on the outside of the circuit as he did so. He finally came to rest just inside the concrete entrance to a tunnel which led to the paddock area. Somehow, he emerged shaken but otherwise unscathed, and with the other Eleven and the Healey out of action, the Seven was pressed into service for Percy to drive in the 1500c sports car race during the Trio meeting at the Kent circuit. After stalling at the start, he powered his way through the pack to place third, and snagged the fastest lap in the process.

The Seven's four-cylinder FWB was then installed in the rebuilt Eleven-Climax for the August Bank Holiday meeting at Brands Hatch, as a new name was added to the team's roster in the form of 'works' Lotus man, Graham Hill. The future double Formula One World Champion and Indy 500 victor was then a mere jobbing wannabe, Warner recalling: "He had talked his way into a job at Lotus Components and we often bought parts from them. He offered to sort out and set up our Lotus Elevens if we would let him drive the Climax-engined car, so we did. At that point in his career he was very determined and very quick, but prone to spinning."

After recording a time of 59.6 sec in practice to eclipse the existing lap record, Hill led the Chequered Flag Trophy race, following a stirring battle in the early stages with future Grand Prix man Alan Stacey. After Stacey spun his Lotus, Hill appeared destined to win the race for its title sponsor, only to get horribly out of shape at Clearways. He returned trackside in third place and moved up to second, only to rotate once again at the same corner in the closing stages. He eventually came home a dejected tenth overall. By way to some conciliation, Percy nursed home the misbehaving Healey – complete with an experimental

Crabb led the *Autosport* race at Goodwood in the Healey 100S during the Whit Monday meeting, only to drop down to an eventual fourth with ignition trouble.

double coil-spring front suspension setup – to fourth place in the production sports car race. Disaster then struck again at Goodwood on August 23 when the seemingly cursed Lotus-Climax – still using the Seven's engine – developed a leaking petrol tank, which obligated Percy to start from the back of the grid. He then made his way up the order only for John Campbell-Jones to spin his Lotus and collect the 'Flag's similar car.

It was, however, patched up in time for September's BRSCC International Meeting at Brands Hatch, with Hill overcoming a detached plug-lead to place second in his heat for the Farningham Trophy contest. Fortuitously, his poor start worked in his favour as the leaders made their way into Druids corner. Chris Bristow had spun his Lotus in the middle of the pack and was collected by several frontrunners. Hill didn't suffer too badly in the multiple-car melee, *Autosport*'s Stuart Seager reporting that "… after being shunted fore and aft, he was making up for lost time and going very fast indeed." Despite his car intermittently lapsing onto three cylinders, Hill finished second behind Alan Stacey.

The Seven's engine was reinstated for the altogether less starry but much-loved Brighton and Hove MC's National Speed Trials a week later, with Warner and mechanic Dave Edwards driving it from Chiswick to the Madeira Drive course where the Seven proved uncharacteristically obstinate along the seafront. "It refused to rev past 6000rpm. The FWB engine had developed a misfire which we thought was probably a fuel feed issue. I'm convinced I could have taken the fastest time of the day had I been able to use the remaining 2200rpm." Even so, Warner still placed second in his class with a time of 29.16 sec over the kilometre course. He would go one better, with fastest time of the day and category honours in the Seven at yet another sprint meeting at Brands Hatch on September 28, only to run out of road in the Healey while trying to shave time and take home further silverware. "I was fine, if slightly sideways, through Druids, but overcorrected on the exit. I then hit the bank halfway down the hill. I dinged one corner rather badly and broke the front suspension: we then had to manhandle it onto a borrowed lorry to get it back to Chiswick."

The giant-slaying Seven, however, covered itself in further glory during a sodden Formula Libre race at Brands, with Percy battling with Formula Two single-seaters – and surviving two lurid spins – en route to a credible fifth place finish. The penultimate meeting for the team witnessed Percy and the lucky Seven beat John Bekaert's HWM-Jaguar to the fastest time of the day at the London Motor Club's sprint at Brands Hatch, inevitably, but this time run anti-clockwise just to keep things interesting. The 'Flag équipe rounded out the season with yet another run at its, by now, regular haunt during the Boxing Day meeting. Percy and the diminutive Seven took the fight to the many single-seaters, which included Graham Hill's Lotus 12, to place fifth overall and claim the concurrent sports car section of the race.

It had been a long time coming, but Warner finally had a season of motorsport under his belt, both as a driver and as a patron. The youthful Chequered Flag Stable had tried hard, often very tryingly, and amid dented cars and bruised egos it had emerged with solid results. Nonetheless, there would be a change of strategy over the winter break. "That year there had been far too many expensive accidents. I decided that from now on I would employ only established professionals, or up-and-coming racers who had some degree of experience; the sort of young charger who had what it took to get the job done."

The era of Warner the talent-spotter had arrived.

One-off Lotus Seven-Climax was campaigned extensively during the team's early years. The car was based in part on the Lotus 12 Formula Two single-seater.

III. Onwards and upwards

Necessity is often the mother of compromise, and The Chequered Flag Stable's sophomore season would involve a degree of rationalisation. Having fielded six cars the previous year, a pragmatic Warner would run just two for 1959: the altogether more important business of selling cars had to take priority. The existing – and proven – Lotus Seven-Climax would be retained, primarily for sprints and hillclimbs with the occasional circuit outing thrown in. Its new stablemate, however, was something altogether more purposeful. Aspirations were elevated with the purchase of a brand new 2-litre Cooper Monaco, which would be shared over the course of the year between Percy Crabb and the team principal.

"Would Sir prefer a Jaguar D-type or an Aston Martin DB3S?" Graham Warner shows racer Mike Dickens a pair of exotic sports-racers.

However, it would be fair to say that the season didn't go quite to plan: this streamlined competition programme slewing off the rails at the first meeting. On March 6, the first ever privately-owned Monaco rolled off the team's transporter at Snetterton for an initial shakedown. Aside from a few teething issues, the Cooper lapped quickly and consistently for more than five hours. A frisson of expectation began to ripple through the team, a sense that was reinforced with successive test sessions at Goodwood and Brands Hatch, where the car proved fast and reliable.

Armed with the Cooper for its maiden outing at Snetterton on March 23, Crabb ventured trackside for qualifying during a torrential downpour. Within three laps he had secured a place on the front row of the grid, only for his good work to be undone the fourth time around. The unfortunate Crabb got into a tank-slapper on the home straight as the Monaco struggled to find traction on the sodden asphalt. He corrected the initial slide, only for the tail to whip round the other way. As Warner recalls, the ensuing accident was catastrophic: "He hit the railway sleepers which lined that part of the circuit and the wreckage was unbelievable. The car completely disintegrated, with bits strewn all over the place. Poor Crabb was concussed and broke his right arm, his collar bone and four ribs. He wasn't in great shape, but it could have been far worse, and obviously we were left somewhat deflated by the whole episode."

With the Cooper reduced to its constituent parts, plans to participate in more prestigious British and international meetings were now in tatters. However, Warner had already added another car to the stable prior to the season opener: "I purchased a Lotus Elite direct from Colin Chapman off Lotus' stand at the 1958 Earls Court Motor Show. It was a replacement for my Porsche 356 Super, and was very much intended as a personal runabout rather than a potential racing car. My Elite, chassis 1006, initially wore the registration number 147VMK and was only the fifth car made."

A remarkably bold design, the Type 14 Elite was the world's first production car to feature an all-glassfibre monocoque, its achingly pretty outline boasting a drag coefficient of just 0.29cd. Similarly left-field, its rev-happy Coventry Climax engine was rooted in a fire pump unit and comprised an alloy block and head. "It had well-balanced handling and fabulous brakes," continues Warner, "but it was too noisy and fussy as a road car; quite delicate, too. The first batch of Elites had their bodies moulded by a boat-building firm in Sussex. The glassfibre was so thin in places you could see fuel sloshing around the petrol tank on a sunny day!"

With The Chequered Flag becoming Lotus distributor for London, campaigning the Elite made sense commercially. Warner and the baby GT car would become inextricably linked: his giant-slaying exploits in time entering into legend. But before the car ever ventured trackside, a degree of fettling was required. "There was a gradual process of refining the car, with Brad Ward ultimately taking over the preparation. He stripped the car and removed 20lb of damp sand from each door! We painted the Elite in 'Flag colours and I debuted it at the same meeting where poor old Percy had his accident."

Just to heap on the misery, Warner was running third behind Sir Gawaine Baillie and 'Gentleman' Jack Sears, only to have a coil break loose. "That shorted out the engine so I came to a complete stop. Our next race was at Snetterton a few weeks later: the engine seized on the first lap."

Two meetings in, and 1959 had thus far amounted to a pair of DNFs, one failure to start, and a very expensive – and uninsured – write-off. After sitting out the Goodwood Easter Meeting, morale was on the floor by the time the équipe turned up at Silverstone on May 2 for the BRDC International Trophy meeting.

This time, however, there would be a marked reversal of fortune. The 1216cc Lotus was entered for the Grand Touring Car race, the quality entry including Stirling Moss in an Aston Martin DB4GT, and the likes of Sears and Roy Salvadori. Lining up on the grid immediately behind Moss, Warner got off to a flier, and by the end of the first lap he was leading his class in a remarkable fourth place overall, despite no prior experience of the full Silverstone circuit. After 12 laps, he came home in seventh place.

Buoyed by this success, the Elite was further tweaked and honed, Warner recalling: "We prepared it by reducing weight wherever possible, removing the bumpers, interior trim and so on. We fitted Borrani wire wheels with larger tyres, twin SUs, then two twin-choke Webers, a special four-branch exhaust, and a close-ratio ZF 'box. Keith Duckworth and Mike Costin of Cosworth improved the engine, rebuilding it many times until it gave a reliable 100-plus bhp: it would pull 8200rpm in top. Dunlop calculated that with the differential ratio and tyres we were using, it was good for more than 140mph. We also reduced air resistance as much as possible by fairing-in the headlights and making Perspex side windows which fitted flush with the door openings."

Warner would dust down the team's faithful Lotus Seven for the Thames Estuary Sprint at Brands Hatch on June 7, its first outing since the previous year's Boxing Day meeting. He came away with class honours; that and a scolded face after a hose burst and sprayed him with hot fluids. Three weeks later, he was leading the Lotus Cars race at the popular Trio meeting, only to be bundled off at Druids on the fourth tour by GK Lambert who, ironically, was driving the ex-Keith Hall/The Chequered Flag Eleven. Then came the Elite's big day, as Warner ventured to Holland in early July for the first ever World Cup GT Match race.

"I had been chatting with the then editor of *Autosport*, Gregor Grant, at the Steering Wheel Club late in 1958. We were both concerned by the lack of suitable races for GT machinery, or rather the sort of cars that people could actually buy and drive on the roads as opposed to the highly specialised sports-racers. The long-distance sports car races such as Le Mans and the 1000km events at Spa, Sebring, Monza, the Nürburgring and Monthléry did have classes for GT cars but these events were way beyond the reach of most amateur and club-level racing drivers. Gregor then suggested that *Autosport* would promote the rather grandiosely titled 'World Cup' series of GT races for national teams. Initially they would be pan-European, but in the hope that it would eventually become a proper worldwide series. I was all for it.

"A few weeks later, Gregor phoned and asked if I could form a British team which would consist of six GT racers, plus a reserve. Some Dutch and German drivers were to do likewise and create their own national squads. Gregor restricted the British team to three Elites, as he wanted a wider spread of marques and drivers. I chose Jim Clark and John Whitmore, both of whom owned quick Lotuses. I'd raced against them several times so I knew they were good. We then had two MGA Twin-Cams which were beautifully prepared by Dick Jacobs. They were to be driven by

Warner bought his Lotus Elite as a road car, ostensibly. He's seen here coming up to lap KA Price's Frogeye Sprite on its race debut.

the 'Flag's Alan Foster and Roy Bloxham. We were further bolstered by the Elva Couriers of Pat Ferguson and Gil Baird.

"Opposition from the Dutch contingent consisted of some very fast Porsche 356s led by Wim Poll, Ben Pon and Gijs van Dijk, but as it happens the Germans didn't register a team. It was left to individual drivers to compete, but they were ineligible for points."

On docking at the Hook of Holland, the British drivers somehow got separated from one another, but each made it to the Zandvoort circuit in time for an improbably warm qualifying session. By the end of the first day, Warner and Clark were comfortably the fastest qualifiers, being the only two drivers to lap in less than two minutes. Whitmore didn't make it to the Netherlands, as his Lotus had been damaged while racing at Monza.

On the afternoon of Sunday July 5, the 60-lap thrash got under way half an hour later than billed. Unfortunately, the cars had been sitting for so long in the searing heat that the fuel in the float chambers of the top two Elites had evaporated: when the flag dropped, both cars were reluctant to start. Clark got away before Warner, but both Lotuses coughed and spluttered for much of the opening tour before finally running cleanly. As the Dutch Porsches made their presence felt up front, Warner overtook 14 cars. Ten laps in, he led Clark for a Lotus one-two and, with 47 laps run and both pit stops completed, he had a clear lap-and-a-half cushion over his pursuers.

While most of the British drivers had retired, including Clark's Elite, it appeared that at least there would be a British overall winner, even if the team prize was history. Then, with the cruellest of luck, a rear hub casting failed on a fast downhill right-hander. Warner was travelling at around 100mph at the time: "The car rolled three times into the dunes. I was unhurt apart from being hit on the back of my helmet by the spare wheel which had worked its way loose. I received two points for recording the fastest lap which I suppose was some consolation. With Pat Fergusson getting ten points as the sole British finisher in fifth place, we left the meeting with just 12 points to the Dutch team's 66. Hans Koch won overall in his Porsche."

The firm's administrator/gofer Mike Beuttler wrote vividly of the team's exploits in *Autosport*, reporting that Warner's fastest lap of 1min 53.7sec "… equalled Belgian Johnny Claes' practice time in a 2.5-litre F1 Ferrari in 1955 and surpassed the average speed of the 1954 Grand Prix won by Ascari in a 2-litre Ferrari."

Remarkably, the Elite had survived its sandy excursion with no structural damage. New parts were flown over the following day and the car was repaired before Warner embarked on a 300 mile dash across Europe to watch the Formula Two race at Rouen before making for Chiswick. The Chequered Flag squad clearly had speed and driver talent in its armoury – all that was lacking was a better finishing record. Despite his insistence that he would not employ staff members to drive for the '59 season, Warner relented in time for the team's next outing: a Sevenoaks and District Club sprint at Brands Hatch where company secretary Dennis St John and Beuttler shared the Seven-Climax, with the latter recording a class win. The boss' plan to keep things simple and run just a pair of cars was also about to come unglued in the biggest possible way.

At the halfway point in the '59 season, The Chequered Flag équipe had little to show for its efforts, but Warner was about to make life exponentially more difficult for himself. More by chance than by planning, he became a racing car constructor. While it wasn't a premeditated scheme, this change of ethos would in time serve to rocket the firm onto the international stage with the 'Flag acting as a launching pad for dozens of future star drivers.

There was also a precedence, Warner having constructed his own car several years earlier. "I built a small sports car which was christened Gemini for no other reason than it was my astrological star sign. I made it for my own use with no thoughts of production. That said, I did have an eye on entering Le Mans and winning the Index of Performance prize. The French organisers used to put the fix in to favour the DB Panhards so it's doubtful that it would ever have happened, besides which it was an impossible dream for a struggling car salesman.

"The Gemini had a 750cc BMW flat-twin engine which was chosen because it was compact, light, well-engineered and surprisingly powerful, and the car emerged weighing less than the German army sidecar and machine gun outfit it came out of. We also used the original shaft drive to the rear differential, the chassis being a ladderframe arrangement with twin braced large diameter tubes. The suspension, alloy wheels and brakes all came from a half-litre Cooper Formula Three car, while cool air from the opening in the nose was ducted straight to the power unit rather than to a heavy water radiator. This system did away with all the usual plumbing and worked very well. I had Williams & Pritchard make the aluminium bodywork. They were real artists and undoubtedly contributed to the British racing car constructors' rise to prominence in the '50s. You could give them little more than a rough sketch on the back of an envelope and they would create something beautiful; something credible. I did a bit better than that for my car, having made a wooden model of it first. The finished car performed well and I think it was forward-looking in its conception and construction, but it took two years to build (1954-56), and I was too busy to use it. I sold the car after 12 months and have no idea what happened to it subsequently."

The nametag would be revived for a new breed of single-seater, Formula Junior having been conceived by Italian nobleman, racer and journalist Count Giovanni 'Johnny' Lurani as a training ground for up-and-coming new drivers. With marques such as Stanguellini at the fore for the maiden '58 season, it was dominated by Italian constructors. However, British interest was aroused in '59 with the Les Redmond-penned Moorland Mk1 being among the first UK designs to venture trackside. The car was briefly run in practice at Snetterton on April 15 by Brian Alderslade, and competed on July 12 at Brands Hatch with EL Hine driving under the John Hine Cars Ltd banner. However, without the means to construct the car in series, former Aston Martin man Redmond approached Warner with an offer: would he like to purchase the production rights? "He came to see me with the prototype on a trailer. It was quite an ugly thing, with a flat letterbox air intake at the front and high tail section – as high as the driver's head – but it piqued my interest."

On July 26, the Elite and the Moorland descended on Snetterton for the Vanwall Trophy meeting, the Lotus melting a piston in practice, the single-seater losing all lubrication from the transfer box in the run-up to the Formula Libre race. An international foray to the daunting AVUS circuit in Germany in support of the German Grand Prix shortly thereafter resulted in another DNF, the Elite's hard-worked engine being riven with cylinder liner problems.

Just to make life that bit more difficult, Warner had entered the revised Moorland Mk2 for the following day's BRSCC August Bank Holiday meeting at Brands Hatch, with Formula 3 regular Ian Raby on driving duties. The London-born garage owner recorded the fastest lap en route to victory in the FJ class. Suitably impressed, Warner reached agreement with Redmond that same month to acquire the manufacturing rights. "The plan was to build six cars under the Gemini banner. We would race two of them and sell the remainder to cover the costs of purchasing the manufacturing rights. We rather underestimated demand!"

And the ramifications for the rest of the business. The acquisition of the Moorland project coincided with

The Moorland Formula Junior was developed into the Gemini Mk2 which featured a heavily revised aluminium body crafted by Williams & Pritchard.

A Chequered Life

The Gemini Mk2 prototype's rear bodywork was much lower and sleeker than the Moorland's.

Beneath the skin, the Gemini Mk2 featured a Speedwell-tuned BMC A-series engine in a spaceframe chassis.

The boss aboard the prototype Gemini Mk2, which was available ready-to-race for £985.

the opening of a new sister showroom in Edgware, run by Alan Foster. With the car sales firm booming, and a competition programme already in place, building single-seaters served only to heap further pressure on Warner. "I had an inkling that Formula Junior was going to be big but I couldn't have foreseen just how big. I got Len Williams at Williams & Pritchard to make a new body for what we called the Gemini Mk2 [briefly Mk1, just to add to confusion …] and placed an advertisement in *Motor Sport* and *Autosport*. By that time Graham Hill was a partner in the Speedwell tuning firm and we did a deal with him to use its tweaked BMC A-series engine in our car. A Gemini ready-to-race could have been yours all in for £985. As soon as the ads appeared we were deluged with orders from all over the world. Of course, we had no prior experience of this sort of thing so we had to get organised in a hurry.

"I was adamant that we were going to do the chassis ourselves so we formed a new company, Chequered Flag Engineering. I didn't want to put chassis out to a subcontractor such as Progress Engineering, which was then one of the bigger players. Your design could be easily copied by a rival and you had no control over build quality. Progress would churn them out for a price, and they certainly did for Lotus. Instead, we set up workshops in the rows of linked lock-up garages behind Cliff Davis Cars in Shepherds Bush. We were fortunate to have a brilliant welder on our side, Roy Thomas, who was better known as 'Tom the Weld.' He was a very hard working chap who also made jigs for the chassis frames."

Les Redmond, Brad Ward, Geoff Rumble, Derek Taylor, and a couple of part-timers constructed the cars.

If Warner wasn't under enough pressure, August 29 marked round two of the *Autosport* World Cup races, this time held at Brands Hatch in the form of two 21-lap heats during the Kentish 100 meeting. To win the overall Cup prize, Team GB needed to clinch the first five places in both heats, and set the fastest lap in one of them. With John Whitmore's Elite now fit and able, it joined the Lotuses of pole-man Warner and Jim Clark on the front row. Each had qualified in the 65 second bracket, and expectations were high. However, a broken diff forced Whitmore to retire, with Clark coming home the winner in the opener from Warner who had lost time following a moment at Kidney Bend. Alan Foster was third in his MGA ahead of Pat Fergusson's Elva. In heat two, the two Elites again ran together, this time with Warner leading

Warner led home fellow Elite driver Jim Clark in part two of the August 1959 *Autosport* World Cup contest at Brands Hatch.

home Clark – taking the fastest lap in the process. It was a great showing for the home side, but the Dutch squad narrowly claimed the series' overall title.

On September 29 of that year the first Gemini was completed, with testing beginning in earnest at Silverstone. It was entered for the October 3 meeting at Brands Hatch, with future Grand Prix occasional Raby once again on driving duties. Matters didn't get off to a flier when a rear upright collapsed during practice, which saw the car launched into a lurid series of spins. The Gemini was repaired overnight, but it was left to rival marque Elva to reap the rewards in the combined F3/Formula Junior race as the Gemini managed only a few laps before a broken propshaft flange prompted retirement.

With only one more meeting left on the team's race card, the following three weeks saw the new Gemini Mk2 put through its paces by a number of drivers, including Geoff Williamson, John Brown, Graham Hill and his Speedwell compatriot Len Adams. The car having lapped Brands Hatch below the existing Formula Junior lap record, all looked rosy. There were, however, one or two additional headaches: the new strain had attracted the attention of PanAm captain Bob Pfaff, who ordered two cars scheduled to be run in the support race the day before the December 12 US Grand Prix. Remarkably, both cars plus the Moorland Mk2 were flown to New York on December 4 and made the race at the Sebring International Raceway circuit in Florida eight days later. Unfortunately, it soon

An elated Warner after besting British and Dutch rivals at Brands Hatch during the *Autosport* World Cup meeting.

became apparent that they were hopelessly undergeared for the long open straights of the bumpy airfield track.

Shortly thereafter, Bill Tannehaueser of Auto Research became the official US distributor, placing orders for 20 cars. Unfortunately, a welding incident caused a fire in the Chequered Flag workshop which, allied to problems with parts supplies, created problems when it came to actually building them. There was also a new, and unanticipated issue – competition from established constructors. With Lotus, Lola and Cooper announcing their intentions to join the Formula Junior ranks, the 'Flag's final meeting of the season at Brands Hatch on Boxing Day would witness a number of new car debuts. Three Geminis were fielded in the John Davy Trophy race, two works entries and Williamson in a privateer car. Warner would drive one, as well as the Elite in the production sports car race, with the other team car being shared by a young Scottish farmer. Then a relative unknown, Jim Clark had shown well aboard his own Lotus, while contesting everything from autotests to big-banger sports car contests in cars ranging from a Goggomobil to a Jaguar D-type. However, while he would go on to become inextricably linked with Lotus, claiming two Formula One driver's titles and the Indianapolis 500 along the way, the Brands Hatch Gemini outing would represent his first ever outing in a single-seater.

His team-mate and entrant Warner recalls it being a trying time for both parties. "At that time the BMC A-series engine was a natural fit for Formula Junior, but that year Ford had announced the new Anglia which had a 997cc 'four'. It had a greater piston area for the same capacity as the BMC unit but with a much shorter stroke so it could rev that much higher. The A-series was limited by the size of the bore and it didn't rev. In my opinion the Anglia engine had huge potential and I thought Keith Duckworth at Cosworth Engineering, which was then a new and very small operation, was the obvious man to take it on. He and his partner Mike Costin had done such a superb job with our Elite and Seven, after all. I then spent a day phoning various departments at Ford's Dagenham plant, trying to find someone who would sell me half a dozen engines. I got passed from pillar to post until eventually someone told me they would be happy to sell me six engines just so long as I bought the cars they came in …

"Obviously that wasn't ideal, and it was clear to me that Ford had zero interest in motorsport which, when you consider its massive investment in the sport across so many disciplines during the '60s, was rather ironic. Shortly thereafter I was driving up the Great West Road in London and went past Lincoln Cars which had the concession for all of Ford's American brands. One of our former salesmen worked there and through him I managed to get an audience with the managing director. I then explained what we wanted and why, showed him photographs of the Gemini and explained why Ford's involvement in racing would be beneficial to its image. He seemed half interested and said he'd get onto Dearborn and give me an answer. A while later he called to say we would have our six engines and they went straight to Duckworth with the intention that we'd have the first race-prepared unit ready for Brands Hatch on December 26. Tom the Weld and the other mechanics then worked all over Christmas installing the engine so we would make the race. I would drive the Ford-engined car, while Jimmy would race the A-series Gemini. I had competed against him several times in Lotuses and knew he was good. I was keen to see how he would get on in a single-seater."

The answer was: not as well as he would have hoped, with Warner also in the wars from the get-go. "The guys had worked their socks off getting the Ford-powered car finished, but in all that rushing about they had forgotten to put the spigot bearing in the middle of the flywheel. I went out in practice and it sounded beautiful. The Ford engine immediately felt nicer than the A-series, but when I opened it up for the first time it went bang and the gearlever started moving around in a stirring motion between my legs. The rear end then locked up and I went backwards and up the backing right in front of the grandstand on the start-finish line. There was no way the car was going to be repairable, but the engine was OK. Colin Chapman was there with the new Lotus 18 'Biscuit Tin' Formula Junior for Alan Stacey to drive. He had also gone for a Ford engine but it wasn't really tuned like ours. They'd had all sorts of problems, too, with the 18 bottoming so badly it had worn away the sump plug. The engine in my car was alright, so I said to Colin that he was welcome to use it. Chapman, Duckworth, Tom the

The Gemini marque participated in its first overseas race in December 1959 during a Formula Junior race at Sebring, organised by the Automobile Club of Florida. Two cars were entered but neither finished.

Weld and our other talented mechanic Chas Beattie then set about taking the engine out of the Gemini and installing it in the Lotus." Stacey would spin off at Bottom Bend in the race while running in seventh place.

"Throughout all this, we had rather neglected poor Jimmy. The A-series Gemini had an electric starter, but no alternator. Shunting the car around had drained the battery so having qualified eighth, it wouldn't start again when he got to the grid. He got a push in order to get moving, but because of that he was later disqualified." Just to make his day complete, Clark then went off at Paddock Hill bend in his Border Reivers Elite while chasing down Warner in the production sports car encounter. The 'Flag rounded out an up-and-down season with a third consecutive victory at Brands Hatch for the Elite, but Warner wasn't able to hold on to Clark for 1960.

"He obviously had a lot of talent. Colin Chapman had also raced against him in Elites and recognised his potential. Lotus was involved in so many difficult formulae, including Formula One, so Chapman dangled all those juicy carrots in front of Jimmy to entice him. I didn't blame him. I can, however, say categorically that I gave Jim Clark his first start in a single-seater and also made the link between Ford and Cosworth, which of course led to the SCA and BDA engines and the legendary DFV, which won 155 Grands Prix. Not every great innovation or significant motor racing milestone back then was down to Chapman!"

IV. The stars align

A guardedly optimistic Graham Warner arrived at a bleak and chilly Snetterton on March 27, 1960 for his first race meeting of the year. At the same setting 12 months earlier, Percy Crabb had comprehensively demolished the team's Cooper Monaco, the Norfolk venue being regarded as a bogey circuit for the Chequered Flag équipe (the Stable part of the name had by now been quietly dropped). Still attired in morning dress after performing best man duties at a friend's wedding, he changed into his race suit before venturing trackside in the Elite as dusk descended. With the Seven-Climax now in the hands of well-known competitor Betty Haig, and the Cooper finally pieced back together and sold off, the little Lotus would be Warner's main weapon of choice for the forthcoming season. Now wearing the registration number LOV1, the Elite went quickest in practice for the production sports car race. The following day, Warner triumphed by 400 yards ahead of the Dick Jacobs-run MGA Twin-Cam, driven by employee Alan Foster.

The Snetterton curse had seemingly been lifted, even if the team's Gemini Mk2 blew a head gasket during practice for the Formula Junior race. Relegated

A racy little number poses with a works Gemini Mk2 at the January 1960 Racing Car Show at Olympia.

Warner enjoyed a stellar 1960 Easter Monday at Brands Hatch, his tiny Elite besting the modified Jaguar XK120 of Dick Gibson in the Grand Touring Car race.

to the third row of the grid, the team principal worked his way up the order to finish third behind the Elva-Auto Unions of Peter Arundell and Chris Threlfall, sharing a new lap record with the former. It was a promising start to the racing year and it was about to get even better. Warner had entered three races for the Easter Monday event at Brands Hatch. He would leave Kent with quite a haul, the subhead to *Autosport*'s report reading "Graham Warner's Field Day at BRSCC Meeting." In the 10-lap Grand Touring Car race, he steered LOV1 to victory ahead of Dick Gibson's modified Jaguar XK120, the same magazine stating that "Warner drove very fast and with absolute precision, building up a handsome lead from Gibson, who was some distance ahead of Brian Whitehouse (Elite)."

Aboard the works Gemini he sealed Formula Junior honours, finishing more than half a lap ahead of Harry Epps' Elva-Auto Union. He then recorded a hat-trick in the 10-lap Formula Junior versus Formula Three scratch race, while also establishing a new category lap record.

With four wins and a third place from five starts, the season had got off to a flier. However, the Snetterton curse returned with a vengeance in time for the next meeting on April 24. The works Gemini entry had to be scratched due to delays getting it prepared, the Elite setting down the fastest lap in practice for the Production Sports Car race only to develop a puncture while sitting on pole position for the race proper. Without sufficient time to change the tyre, the Lotus was consequently pit-bound for its first DNS of the season.

Gemini production was also threatening to overextend the team as demand from North America

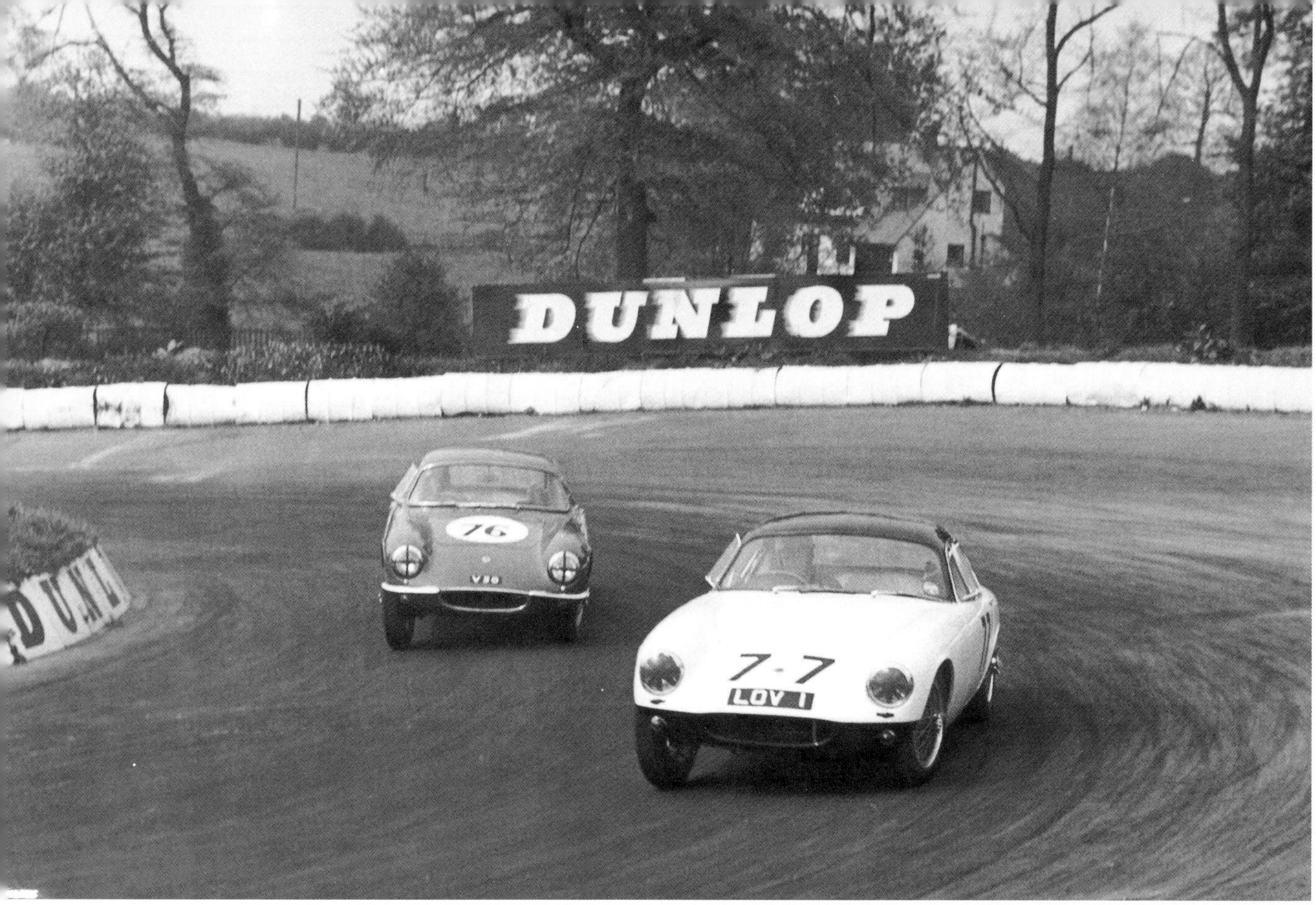
DUNLOP
76
7-7
LOV 1

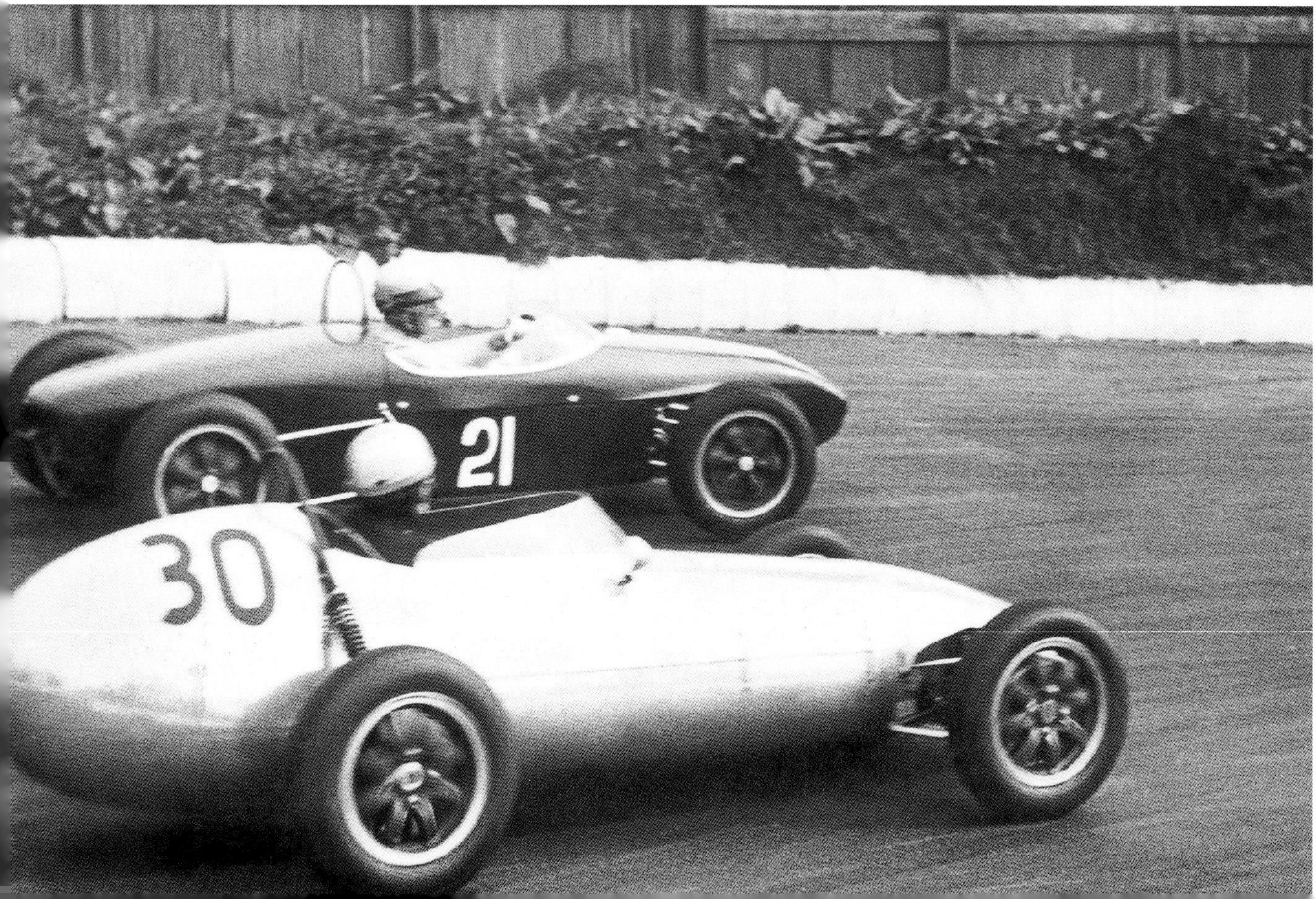
21
30

Left: The Elites of Warner and Tommy Dickson were never far apart in the GT race at Mallory Park in early May 1960, with Dickson just getting the nod. Bottom left: Warner finished third in the Formula Junior race at Mallory Park in May 1960. His Gemini is seen here battling the Lotus 18 of fourth-place finisher, Eric Bantlin.

in particular outstripped supply. Even a seasoned multi-tasker such as Warner was a little overwhelmed by the reaction to the car. "It soon started to get out of hand. We used several workshops from which to build the cars: the main one was a row of open-plan lock-ups behind Cliff Davis Cars in Shepherds Bush until Davis – who was a bit of a rogue, to put it mildly – doubled the rent. We also used two Railway Arches at Turnham Green, the small workshop at the rear of the original Chiswick showrooms, and then later on in the Gemini story we leased a small factory in Wales Farm Road off the Western Avenue. In the early days we had complications caused by outside suppliers failing to deliver on promises. It also didn't help that customers kept changing their orders; altering the spec of their cars. But most of all, 1960 witnessed major changes in racing car design, which we had to respond to. We also had significantly greater competition from other constructors relative to when I took on the Moorland less than a year earlier."

Nonetheless, Warner the racing driver continued from where he left off at Silverstone on April 30 for the Maidstone & Mid Kent meeting, winning the *Autosport* Championship Class B & C race from pole position despite robust opposition during the opening laps from Elva Courier man, Chris Meek. Armed with a brand new Gemini for the Formula Junior race, Warner made it as far as Becketts on his out lap during practice: oil leaked onto the tyres, which prompted a grassy excursion. With a new sump in place for the start, he came through a thin field to finish second behind Jack Cordingley's Elva 100.

Venturing to Mallory Park on May 8 for the BRSCC meeting, Warner made a blistering start from fourth on the grid for the GT race to power into the lead. An epic scrap ensued with Tommy Dickson's similar Elite, the battle going down to the wire as the two Lotuses were rarely more than half a car length apart. The order was settled for good on the final tour when Warner fluffed a gear change at the hairpin, Dickson inflicting a rare defeat on LOV1 as he held on to the line. At the same meeting the 'Flag took home another third place in the Formula Junior encounter, Warner splitting the Lotus hordes.

Then came the BRDC's Silverstone International Trophy Meeting on May 13. The Elite was due to run in the GT race, only for the clutch to begin slipping in practice. This was followed shortly thereafter by a sudden drop in oil pressure. With the main bearings now history, the Lotus was parked. In the 25-lap Formula Junior event, the 'Flag was represented by three Geminis, with Warner being joined by Australian Tom Hawkes, who had been competing since 1947, and motorcycle legend Geoff Duke. With six world championship titles to his name on two wheels, the 37-year-old had prior experience of racing on four with the works Aston Martin team in 1953. News of his return to racing cars was trumpeted in the sporting weeklies, with *Autosport* reporting: "He selected the Gemini from several offers and has lapped Oulton Park at times comparable with those of John Surtees."

Warner had been impressed by Duke ever since his partial season with Aston Martin: "He was an excellent driver and better than Mike Hailwood who also made the switch from motorcycles to cars. In my view he was almost as good as John Surtees, and a potential world champion if he'd had the right car."

Nonetheless, that first meeting ended with a middling seventh, eighth and tenth place finishes for the 'Flag out of 14 finishers, Jim Clark edging out Surtees for the win.

It was becoming increasingly clear that the Gemini Mk2 was fast becoming obsolete, as mid-engined rivals, most obviously from Elva and Lotus, were clear frontrunners. Nonetheless, the 'Flag's next outing was the prestigious Formula Junior Grand Prix in Monaco. Problems arose before the squad left England. As team member Mike Beuttler recalled in *Autosport*: "The main party, with the three cars, was to leave on the Monday and travel down by road, arriving on Wednesday morning with practice being on the Thursday and Friday. Unfortunately, when they reached Dover they found they had no tickets. This was not, to be quite honest, completely their fault as I had locked them up in a drawer and forgotten about them! However, that little local difficulty was soon surmounted by giving the Port Authorities a personal cheque, going quickly aboard and sailing for Boulogne, hoping all the way to Monaco that the cheque wouldn't bounce!"

He went on to add: "Competition for the Formula Junior race was stiff. We learned that there had been over 150 applicants for entries, and although the best 50 had been accepted, only 22 would be allowed to

Australian driver Tom Hawkes, seen here ahead of Graham Warner, failed to qualify his works-entered Gemini for the May 1960 Monaco Formula Junior race.

start! Practising sessions were therefore split into two halves, with 25 cars in each: this meant that there was roughly half the original time available, as well as the contestants being among the best in Europe. It was a serious business. Apart from having to qualify, no starting money at all was paid – prize money only – therefore not only did one have to go fast enough in practice, but finish well up in the actual race. Geoff Duke and Graham Warner both qualified in Ford-engined cars, but unfortunately Tom Hawkes, in his own BMC-engined car, failed by a heartbreakingly small margin.'

The race itself proved a disaster. Neither Warner nor Duke had practiced with full tanks, and the extra weight made its presence felt on the opening lap as Warner spun coming on to the seafront. A lap later Duke was wrong-footed by the adverse camber on the run to Casino and also spun. Having qualified ninth, he undid his good work and stalled the car, which was by now lying crossways in the middle of the track, with Tim Parnell striking the barriers in avoidance in his Lotus before scorching from 21st place to eighth at the flag. Warner, meanwhile, managed to get going again, only to endure another spin at Tabac corner on the third tour. He would come home an embattled and dejected

Warner finished an embattled fifteenth in the principality following a trying race in his Gemini-Ford.

fifteenth overall. "It wasn't a great meeting for us, that's for sure. That said, Hawkes failed to qualify but he paid most of the transportation costs, which was something. It really was a case of it never rains, but it pours."

If was about to get even more inclement, as further dramas lay ahead in the principality. As Beuttler recalled in *Autosport*: "After the Grand Prix for F1 cars on the Sunday everyone relaxed and we were very sorry to have to leave on Monday. In fact, one of the Geminis decided that it didn't wish to leave at all, and going down the very steep hill into the town came off its trailer and careened away, heading for various vehicles parked by the side of the road. Sure enough it collected one, a Peugeot, and came to a crunching halt. Regrettably, the owner just so happened to be passing at that precise moment and we were treated to a magnificent tirade of French abuse."

With an entente cordial brokered with the aggrieved Peugeot owner, Warner and the 'Flag squad returned to the UK. The boss then finished second at Mallory Park in the Elite and followed this with a BRSCC meeting at Brands Hatch on July 3. Tony Maggs was entered in the lead car with Beuttler driving the sister entry. Maggs placed second behind Lotus man Peter Ellis, with Beuttler proving reasonably quick right up until retirement on the twelfth lap. He wrote in *Autosport*: "I had to retire when third on the eleventh lap with an expensive hole in the side of the block where a rod had emerged for some fresh air."

The team principal, however, was in Zandvoort for a return run of the *Autosport*-backed World Cup match contest. The first leg was held in Holland with Team GB consisting of three Elites driven by Warner, Chris Summers, and John Whitmore (the latter borrowing a car from the Chequered Flag); two pale green Dick Jacobs MGAs driven by Alan Foster and Tommy Bridger, and the rapid Austin-Healey Sebring Sprite of Paddy Gaston. The local contingent had the legs on the British opposition in practice, with Gerhard Koch fastest ahead of Dutch team leader and fellow Porsche man Wim Poll, with Warner third quickest. However, two bad accidents marred practice with Dutchman Harry Kiviet surviving a roll in his Elite at the same spot where Piers Courage would perish in the Dutch Grand Prix a decade later. German Karl Braun, meanwhile, was seriously injured after crashing his Porsche 356 Carrera.

Having been the last to leave the grid a year earlier as intense heat evaporated the fuel in his Lotus' carburettors, Warner would not make the most rapid of getaways in 1960 either. Following the traditional Le Mans start sprint to the car, he chose to fasten his harness before leaving the line, mindful of what had happened in the build-up to the race. The 'safety first' mantra would come home to roost early on after Gaston rolled his Sprite down a steep bank, fortunately without incurring injury. Then it all began to unravel for LOV1. The Elite had been brimmed with fuel to last the 120-mile race distance, with lap times tumbling as the tank emptied. All competitors were obliged to perform a compulsory pit stop to take on a gallon of petrol from a sealed can. Somehow, Warner emerged trackside with a completely full tank, much to the detriment of his lap times. Circulating two seconds-a-lap slower than before he had pitted, he was unable to make up the deficit to eventual winner, Poll. Koch was second ahead of Warner, with Dan Dijk fourth, Foster fifth and Bridger sixth. After the opening bout, Holland led Team GB by a mere two points.

No sooner was the Elite back in England than it was in the thick of it at Snetterton Motor Racing Club's Archie Scott Brown Memorial Trophy meeting on July 8. And, once again, it was a Porsche that provided the stiffest competition. Martyn Watkins reported in *Autosport*: "Event four was for touring and grand touring cars, and pole position on the grid was occupied by Graham Warner's very fast Lotus Elite … Warner was first into the Riches Corner, followed closely by [Marcos driver] Bill Moss and Dickie Stoop's enormously fast Porsche. Warner managed to retain his lead for the rest of the race but was never secure, with Stoop challenging at every opportunity. Lap after lap the cars crossed the start and finish line almost side by side, both drawing well away from third place man Moss who was by now engaged in a furious dice with David Hobbs' Jaguar."

Unfortunately, Warner hadn't been quite so fortunate in the preceding race for Formula Juniors. After stalling on the grid, he was overtaken by the swarming pack before putting on a comeback charge on a damp track. However, with the hard work done, he was forced to retire with an overheating engine. The sister car of Beuttler, meanwhile, fared little better. Displaying his relative inexperience, Beuttler out-braked himself at the Esses and had to take to the escape road.

The works Geminis didn't cover themselves in glory during their next outing at Silverstone for the British Grand Prix support race, either. After being besieged with niggling problems in practice, third row starter Geoff Duke was running fourth early on, battling with Mike McKee's Lotus, only for the clutch to start slipping. Retirement beckoned. Warner's sister car developed a mystery engine ailment in sympathy, resulting in a distant eleventh place finish.

A day later Warner was at Brands Hatch for The Lord's Taverners meeting, driving the Elite in the Grand Touring Car race. It was the indecently quick Triumph TR3 of Colin Hextall which made it to Paddock first, with LOV1 moving ahead four laps in. Warner held on to win ahead of Brian Woodhouse's Elite with Formula Three legend Don Parker taking advantage of Hextall's late race pirouette at Druids to annex third place aboard his Jaguar XK150. In the Formula Junior race, Warner was forced to retire on the final lap, following a spirited race-long battle with Ian Raby's Envoy and Chuck Dietrich's Elva. Contact was made as they attempted to lap a backmarker, with the Gemini and the Envoy being damaged in the ensuing melee.

Meanwhile, in Chiswick, work continued apace on an all-new Formula Junior design. The Gemini Mk2 was clearly no longer a frontrunner as rear-engined designs began to make their presence felt. In early 1960 work began on the new Mk3. The new design comprised a spaceframe chassis with the customary Ford-Cosworth engine mounted amidships, allied to a Renault-derived gearbox. Warner recalls: "I laid out the design, working with our engineers Tom the Weld and Geoff Rumble, both of whom went on to design and build cars of their own [under the Titan and Dastle banners respectively]. Following my experiences driving the Gemini Mk2 with its rear-mounted fuel tank, I mounted pannier-type tanks low on either flank of the Mk3 in-line with the centre of gravity and dropped down wheel seizes from 15in to 13in to lower unsprung weight – the use of inboard rear brakes also helping – and also to reduce the size of the whole car. The rear suspension used a wide-based lower wishbone that was centrally pivoted, using the fixed-length driveshafts as the upper wishbone, with the alloy hub carriers being located fore and aft by twin radius rods."

Debuting at the August Bank Holiday Silver City Trophy meeting, the Mk3 failed to cover itself in glory. With Warner and 'Flag returnee Tony Maggs armed with works Mk2s, it was left to John Whitmore to showcase the team's new challenger. The future European Touring Car Champion struggled to accommodate his 6ft 2in frame into the small single-seater, and spun off two laps into the Formula Junior race on the new long circuit after failing to sufficiently articulate his feet within the tight pedal box. After an off-circuit moment at Druids, he got going again for an eventual tenth place. It was hardly an auspicious start for the team's 'brave new world,' and neither Warner nor Maggs finished the race in the older design. According to *Autosport*'s cryptic analysis, this was due to "... bad preparation." Just to add salt to the wound, LOV1 threw a tantrum in the Wrotham Trophy race for GT cars, Warner retiring the Lotus on the opening lap with a broken crankshaft and a corresponding hole in the engine block.

The timing of this breakage could not have been more inopportune, as a week later LOV1 was due to anchor the British squad for the return leg of the *Autosport* World Cup Match contest, this time at Snetterton on August 5. It was only following a Herculean effort by Keith Duckworth that the Lotus was up-and-running in time for the meeting, which comprised two 20-lap races with a combined distance of 110 miles. With Whitmore unavailable, Pat Fergusson re-joined the Team GB line-up with his Elva, the squad otherwise remaining unchanged from the previous round at Zandvoort.

Despite question marks over LOV1's engine, which was only completed at 4am on the morning of the tournament, Warner wasn't to be denied victory in the opener. With the Dutch visitors unable to field two cars following breakages in practice, the previous year's overall winners were already on the backfoot. Warner came home the victor ahead of Tommy

Bridger's MGA Twin-Cam and Dutchman Wim Poll's Porsche. The second instalment wouldn't be so clear cut, as Warner and Poll became embroiled in an epic race-long duel. David Pritchard gushed in *Autosport*: "In 20 laps of breathtaking struggle, the Elite and the Porsche were seldom more than two lengths apart and the fight was absolutely clean from start to finish … The two leaders tore around the final lap as though tied together and, as they came out of Coram Curve and through Paddock Bend to the finishing straight, Poll made a supreme effort which failed by no more than half a length. A wonderful race was over; Graham Warner had completed a fine job of work for the British team and won for himself the magnificent Samengo-Turner Trophy, Wim Poll had earned the Les Leston Award which took the form of a crash-hat, and Tommy Bridger and [Porsche driver] Ad Bouwmeister had filled the next two places with great credit."

With just enough time to catch his breath, Warner's next outing was at Goodwood on August 20 for the Tourist Trophy meeting. With LOV1 entered in the 1300cc class, Maggs was recalled to active service in the Gemini Mk3 for the BARC International Formula Junior Championship support race. The Rhodesian impressed in qualifying, his time of 1min 35sec ensuring a front row grid slot between Lotus man Trevor Taylor and Elva charger Peter Arundell. The opening heat, however, would prove maddening for the 'Flag faithful Gemini as the starter motor refused to engage at the off. Maggs was swallowed whole by the rest of the field, only getting going following a push-start. He then put on a display of controlled aggression, bettering the existing Formula Junior lap record, but to no avail. His efforts counted for nothing as he was disqualified for receiving outside assistance at the start. Trevor Taylor won on aggregate from Lotus team-mate Jim Clark.

Warner's run in the 108-lap Tourist Trophy proved equally exasperating. With six similar Elites also running in the 1300cc class, including the proven entries of Tommy Dickson and Rootes engineer Mike Parkes, honours were far from assured. First practice witnessed a constant misfire at high revs, followed shortly thereafter by complete electrical failure. The second practice session was more productive, with LOV1 qualifying in fourteenth place overall and fourth in class. Parkes was comfortably fastest and tore into an early lead. Dickson was soon out following a crash at Woodcote, with Parkes heading the Elite of Chris Summers during the early running. An hour in, Parkes

Despite problems with his Lotus' engine in the run-up to the meeting, Warner emerged victorious in the August 1960 *Autosport* World Cup races at Snetterton.

A garlanded Warner smiles as champagne is poured into the Samengo-Turner Trophy which he received for winning the *Autosport* World Cup mini-series.

led the 1300cc runners by more than a minute, holding what appeared to be an unassailable lead over fellow Lotus runner Peter Lumsden, who now held second place with Warner closing in on his tail. At three-quarter distance, LOV1 moved ahead, only for Lumsden to retake the position three laps later amid squabbling backmarkers. Then, with only two laps left to go, Parkes suffered the cruellest of luck as a left-hand side rear tyre burst as he exited Lavant Corner. Lumsden and Warner were now battling for category honours. On the final tour, Warner momentarily got alongside Lumsden, only for the gap between the two warring Elites to abruptly narrow. As a consequence of this, LOV1 bounced off the scenery, with Lumsden holding on for the class win. Warner managed to get going again, the front end of his Lotus now badly damaged, and somehow overcame a broken steering arm to limp over the line for second place ahead of Summers and a recovering Parkes.

The following week was spent gluing LOV1 back together, only for Elite to take another hefty hit at the next race on the long circuit at Brands Hatch for the Kentish 100 meeting, except this time it would be at the opposite end. The bothersome misfire had returned during practice, which relegated Warner to the fourth row of the grid. Running eleventh at the end of the first lap, he was soon up to fifth as the misfire cleared, only to be forced to brake hard halfway around Bottom Bend in avoidance of another car. He, in turn, was thumped by the AC Ace-Bristol of Bill McCowan just after the bridge at South Bank Bend. A battered LOV1 returned trackside to finish sixth overall, with its beleaguered pilot sharing a new class record with Mike Parkes by way of some consolation.

Worse was to come. By now production of the Gemini Mk2 had ended, with Mike Beuttler taking in selected club races in a front-engined car without much in the way of success. The main thrust for the 'Flag was the Mk3 prototype, which in early September '60 was crashed heavily at a Silverstone test day. This put-paid to further racing until the October 1 British Empire Trophy meeting at the Northamptonshire venue, with Geoff Duke reinstated to drive the newly rebuilt Gemini. Cooper driver Henry Taylor was on imperious form all weekend, leading the Formula Junior contest from start to finish in appalling conditions. Peter Arundell placed second, although Duke was closing in on him in the closing stages, only to hit standing water at Maggots Curve and aquaplane into a ditch.

It was still lashing it down for the GT race. With the

Elite back in one piece, Warner planted it on pole, but it was the second row-starting 3.8-litre Jaguar XK120 of Dick Gibson that arrived at Copse Corner first. With cars leaving the circuit at every turn, Warner survived a second lap spin at Club Corner, but dropped from second place to sixth. On a sodden track, he made his way back up the order to finish second by a car's length as Gibson triumphed.

Returning to Snetterton in early October, The Chequered Flag team was first compelled to overcome all manner of obstacles. With many roads becoming flooded en route from Chiswick to Norfolk, some were clearly impassable. Just to compound the problem, the trailer containing the Elite developed three punctures during the journey. If this hadn't livened things up sufficiently, the much-derided transporter containing two Geminis was on hand to provide additional drama. Still some 70-or-so miles shy of Snetterton, it threw a conrod before momentarily catching fire. It was abandoned in a layby on the A11, with the boss and Mike Beuttler returning to Chiswick to find two cars and as many trailers with which to tow the stricken Formula Juniors. Following a high-speed thrash in perilous conditions, both Geminis somehow made it to Snetterton in time for practice. Beuttler in particular had a vested interest in ensuring this was so, as he was down to race the older Mk2. He would ultimately finish ninth.

Star turn, however, was Tony Maggs in the Mk3 prototype. After qualifying on pole, he undid all of his good work at the start by selecting neutral. Engulfed by the 30-strong pack, he fought his way through the order to take the lead on the final tour, bagging the fastest lap in the process. It marked a breakthrough for a design which had promised much but had, until now, delivered little. In failing light, Warner rounded out the day with another tussle with Gibson's modified Jaguar in the shortened GT encounter. Try as he might, he couldn't find a way past, although a new class lap record provided some comfort.

However, it would be third time lucky for Warner at Brands Hatch for the Lewis-Evans Meeting on October 21. Warner had his revenge in the GT support race on the Club circuit, vanquishing Gibson to finish ahead of the well-driven Morgan of second place man Chris Lawrence. Hopes for a repeat win in the Formula Junior thrash were bolstered when Tony Maggs in the Mk3 annexed pole position alongside Jim Clark and Peter Arundell in the works Lotus 18s, a move which flattered to deceive. Clark would lead home his Lotus team-mate – both performing considerably better in the race than in qualifying. Maggs finished a distant third overall, someway clear of Peter Ellis' Lotus.

Following an up-and-down campaign, The Chequered Flag would draw a veil over its third season in the best way possible at the popular BRSCC Boxing Day meeting at Brands Hatch. Peter Ashdown joined the roster to drive the Mk3, with Mike Parkes on hand to debut the new slimmer and stiffer Mk3A, which had been built from scratch in just four weeks. Warner was keen to give both drivers a chance, opining: "I had watched Ashdown in sports cars and he was clearly very good. I thought he had a lot of talent. He was certainly in line for a regular drive with us but he was great friends with Eric Broadley at Lola which ultimately scuppered this. Mike, on the other hand, was

Pole-sitter Tony Maggs engaged the wrong gear at the start of the October 1960 Formula Junior race at Snetterton, but tore through the field to win aboard the prototype Gemini Mk3.

exceptional. He was a natural and good in anything, whether it was a Ferrari GT car, a Jaguar saloon or a single-seater. His day job was designing what became the Hillman Imp and his father was the chairman of Alvis. I can recall all of us all going out for lunch together one day in one of the firm's six-wheeled Saracen armoured personnel carriers. We didn't have trouble parking … I thought Mike would have the necessary blend of ability and technical understanding to evaluate the car and to bring it forward. He also had prior experience of racing single-seaters with the strange little Fry-Climax in which he'd gone quite well.

"We had made the Mk3 prototype a bit too small for taller drivers, though, so enlarged the cockpit on the production 3As which also had glassfibre bodies. We soon had specially cast front wheels with integral brake liners rather than a separate brake drum. Mike was rather on the lofty side, though, and still struggled to fit in the new car. Even so, it didn't seem to slow him down."

However, there would be no dream debut win for the latest Gemini. Parkes' gearlever broke loose on the second lap, forcing him to change gear with the residual stump. Despite this obvious handicap, he still managed to finish third, just two seconds behind Arundell. Ashdown, meanwhile, had problems of his own with a slipping clutch blunting his challenge. Nonetheless, he still managed to come home a credible fourth overall. The team chief then ended his personal campaign in style with another win and fastest lap aboard LOV1 in the GT & Production Sports Car race.

On balance it had been a successful season, but it had come at considerable cost. The racing programme had been largely funded by the core business. However, there had been a noticeable drop-off in car sales due to the government's imposition of much tougher hire purchase restrictions. The Gemini project had also been a major drain on resources, resulting in a net loss for The Chequered Flag of £14,000 which would be more than £200,000 in today's money. For 1961, the team would be underwritten in part by Esso, with the boss digging deep to cover the shortfall.

Warner and LOV1 chased down the famous LawrenceTune Morgan of Chris Lawrence to win the GT support race at Brands Hatch in October 1960.

V. Supply and demand

Running a motor racing team isn't the most obvious route to riches, as Graham Warner would attest: the 1960 season having been, for the most part, personally underwritten. Now armed with Dunlop backing and limited support from Esso, and with the car sales business returning to prosperity, The Chequered Flag team would consolidate its position as a major player at national level in '61. Warner the driver was also about to enjoy a stellar season of his own. There were, however, one or two distractions for Warner the team principal.

"I was kept occupied, that's for sure. I was at the Chiswick showroom until 7pm most days. I visited the Edgware showrooms weekly and the one in Nottingham monthly. I enjoyed being busy, but then in March '61 Charlie Kolb won the Sebring International Formula Junior race in the prototype Gemini Mk3. He had originally approached us about running a car for him, as he thought the Gemini was much better than his Elva. Although I'd heard he was a quick driver, and was naturally keen to see him in a Gemini, we said we couldn't get involved in running one in the States, so he acquired the car from us instead."

Kolb beat a quality field in the Sebring 12 Hours support race which included the likes of the Rodríguez brothers Pedro and Riccardo, Walt Hansgen, and Jim Hall. He did so emphatically, starting from pole position

Running the 'Flag kept Warner busy as sports car sales blossomed, but demand for Geminis was about to cause a few headaches.

and recording the fastest lap en route to victory. Warner was pleased, if not entirely surprised by the result: "I knew it was a good design and a competitive car. We were now pushing on with the Mk3A but beating the Coopers, Lotuses, Lola, Stanguellinis and so on in the US meant there was unforeseen extra demand which we had to meet."

Even more so after Kolb and his Mk3 won the Governors Cup race at Marlboro Raceway in Maryland on April 16. "Following Kolb's success, we were flooded with orders from the US. Then a chap called Bob Johnson came on the scene. He may have financed the Mk3 for Kolb; I'm not sure of their relationship. Johnson, who had replaced Tannehauser as the US Gemini distributor, funded the purchase, and the car was run under the Gemini Racing Cars banner. What I do know is that he persuaded me that his operation, rather than Kolb's, would be a more efficient sales outlet in the US if we granted him the sole Gemini concession. We did just that, and about nine or ten months later he disappeared."

Closer to home, the works Mk3A would prove fast, the real issue being its finishing record. On March 19, a week before the Sebring race, Warner and the 'Flag squad descended on Norfolk for the Snetterton Spring Meeting with the team chief armed with his trusty Lotus for the 8-lap Grand Touring Car race. The sole factory Gemini Mk3A was entered for Peter Ashdown who had already signed for Lola and was onside for just this one meeting. Despite losing third gear early on, he nursed the car home in third place in the 10-lap Formula Junior thrash. Warner, meanwhile, started the year as he meant to continue with a decisive victory aboard the Elite.

The following weekend saw the équipe back at Snetterton for the SMRC International Lombank Trophy meeting, Warner again equipped with LOV1, with two Geminis being fielded for Mike Parkes and Bill McCowen. The latter signing raised more than a few eyebrows in qualifying, defying his inexperience with single-seaters to record a practice lap of 1min 43.8sec. Warner had been impressed with his form in sports cars the previous season, and was keen to see how he would get on in an open-wheeler. "I had seen him race at Goodwood, and he was a good driver, but sometimes he would get a bit carried away and spin off."

The AC Ace-Bristol regular kept it together this time around, though, and qualified on the front row for his Formula Junior debut. He would finish eighth following a measured drive. His team-mate, however, endured a torrid time. The engine in Parkes' car refused to run cleanly in practice and was changed the night before the race. This second engine was then found to have the wrong camshaft, with Mike Beuttler returning to Chiswick to pick up another Cosworth unit bound for a customer's car. This was installed by noon of race day, but the mechanics' herculean efforts were for nought as the clutch began to slip early on in the race. Parkes came home a dejected eleventh overall.

Warner, meanwhile, was in the wars during practice for the GT race. Oversized rear tyres put extra strain on the transmission under braking, which caused a bearing to break. With a quick fix in place for the race, Warner was doubtful that it would complete the 12-lap distance. However, pre-race bodges defied expectations and it held together to the end: Warner came home fourth overall and first in the up to 2000cc class with the expected threat from Mike McKee's new UDT-Laystall Elite failing to materialise. Overall winner was the ever-adaptable Parkes aboard Tommy Sopwith's Ecurie Endeavour Ferrari 250GT SWB.

Parkes was now on board for the season as a factory Gemini driver. The second seat, however, remained vacant. For the following meeting, the major Easter Monday event at Goodwood on April 3, Geoff Duke was due to return to the fold and compete in the Chichester Cup race. Warner was eager to sign him for the year, but business commitments ultimately meant the motorcycle star didn't make it to West Sussex. Warner stood in at short notice, his race ending before it began after his Mk3A developed an oil leak on the grid. Parkes, meanwhile, made a perfect getaway, only to be taken out by Alan Rees, whose rotating Lotus came to a halt with the Gemini teetering on top of it.

Once again it was left to LOV1 to save face for the 'Flag, Warner beating McKee for class honours and fifth place overall in the 10-lap Fordwater Trophy encounter. This race also witnessed the first of many skirmishes with Les Leston who was debuting his new Elite DAD10. A week later, Warner would take another win at Snetterton only to round out the month with a non-start at Oulton Park for the BARC meeting where Graham Hill claimed a debut win for the new Jaguar E-type. Having travelled all the way to Cheshire from Chiswick without a murmur, the Lotus' gearbox seized in practice. A replacement transmission was dispatched from London – via an aeroplane – but it failed to arrive in time.

Misfortune also rained abundant on the two-car Gemini team. Duke was back on board at the same meeting, but was spooked by an unfamiliar car which, it later transpired, was hopelessly over-geared. Parkes, meanwhile, struggled after his car became stuck in top gear at the start of his Formula Junior heat. Having nursed it for much of the running, the throttle cable

Mike Parkes endured a torrid Formula Junior race at Silverstone in April 1961, his Gemini coming to rest on top of Alan Rees' Lotus following contact.

LOV1 was the class of the field in the GT race at the BRSCC Lord's Taverners meeting at Brands Hatch in May 1961, only to retire on the penultimate lap after it threw a con-rod.

snapped in the closing stages, which ended his run permanently. As *Autosport* observed, somewhat unnecessarily, "He was not in the least bit amused."

Warner, meanwhile, was gifted the opportunity to sample a rival's car at the April 23 BRSCC meeting at Brands Hatch. UDT Laystall's team boss, Ken Gregory ,asked Graham to test its Elite, which in turn became an opportunity to race the Lotus. However, after lapping the short circuit some four seconds slower than he'd managed on the same track in his own car, he politely declined Gregory's offer. "McKee didn't like it at all, and it certainly wasn't as well balanced as LOV1, so I made a few suggestions which did improve the car."

Hopping back into his usual machine, he batted away Gordon Jones' Marcos-Climax and Peter Lumsden's Lotus to win the sports car race by a whisker.

Unfortunately, the team's miserable luck returned with a vengeance at the sodden BRDC International Trophy meeting at Silverstone on May 6. In the Formula Junior encounter, Parkes' race lasted just five laps before the clutch let go. The sister car, which for one race was entrusted to Mike Beuttler, retired after a chunk of the timing chain broke off and fell into the sump. The result was a damaged oil pump and another costly DNF. The following day saw Warner return to Brands Hatch, but hopes of a repeat win were dashed on the penultimate lap when LOV1 threw a rod while leading the similar cars of David Hobbs and Les Leston. A new lap record was scant consolation.

A fortnight and several around-the-clock rebuilds later, the 'Flag arrived at Crystal Palace for the Whitsun Monday meeting. The 15-lap Norbury Trophy race witnessed another battle with Leston's Elite, the paucity of love between the two Lotus protagonists

bubbling over as the season progressed. At the London venue, LOV1 moved ahead of DAD10 for class honours on the fourth tour, only to be baulked by an oblivious backmarker on the final corner of the last lap. Sometime Grand Prix driver Leston (born Alfred Lazarus Fingleston) was able to nip by to triumph by half a car's length.

The same meeting also marked the arrival of WF 'Bill' Moss as a works Gemini racer, Warner having been impressed with his handling of a self-run Lotus 18 earlier in the season. "He was a very nice chap, a good driver and someone who I thought had potential to go further. I first became aware of him when he was racing an ancient ERA that Prince Bira of Siam had driven prior to WWII. I thought if Moss could drive something like that, and drive it well, he should be able to adapt to a Gemini. As it happens, Bill slotted in to the team very nicely."

While a debut win for the new signing was asking a lot, he more than repaid Warner's faith with a fine fourth place finish in the Anerley Trophy race. Parkes, meanwhile, finished second behind Alan Rees following a stellar recovery drive. Formula Three star-turned-race driving school proprietor Jim Russell went off on the third lap, his car smacking into the retaining wall and losing a wheel in the process. Fourth place man Parkes spun in avoidance, and had to watch half the pack stream past before he could rejoin the fray. The Gemini team leader tore through the pack, establishing a new Formula Junior lap record as he did so, but ran out of time in his bid to catch Rees.

The Mk3 prototype's wins at Sebring and Marlboro by now seemed a long time ago, the winless works effort with the Mk3A having been hobbled as much by a lack of reliability as adversity. If nothing else, Parkes' performance at Crystal Palace showcased the car's raw pace. At the next meeting at Brands Hatch on June 3, it would be proven beyond all doubt.

While Stirling Moss claimed the headline 200 mile Silver City International Trophy encounter, the unrelated Bill Moss was on victorious form in the John Davy Trophy support race. With a strong entry for the high-profile Formula Junior thrash on the full-length 2.6 mile circuit, pole-sitter Parkes led at the off from works Lotus man Trevor Taylor, with Moss holding station in third place. Taylor slipped past on the third tour and led the Gemini duo for the next 12 laps, building up a six second cushion over his pursuers. Parkes' car then intermittently refused to pull cleanly which allowed Moss through into second. Then on the approach to Druids, the engine in Taylor's car died momentarily, which was all the incentive Moss and the recovering Parkes needed. Both Geminis pounced on the stricken Lotus, with Moss leading Parkes home by 3.8sec for an emotional one-two result for the 'Flag.

The line-astern finish was the icing on a highly calorific cake for a team that had endured so many frustrating weekends during the first half of the

Left: Warner led the GT race at the 1961 Whitsun Trophy meeting at Crystal Palace, only to lose out to arch-rival Les Leston on the final lap after being baulked by a backmarker.

Former ERA tamer Bill Moss joined the 'Flag team for the May '61 Whitsun Trophy meeting. He finished fourth in his Gemini Mk3A as team leader Mike Parkes emerged victorious.

season. Earlier in the day, Warner had emerged top of his class during the 10-lap Peco Trophy GT race. As Parkes came home the outright winner in Major Ronnie Hoare's Ferrari, fellow front-row starter Warner withheld a sustained attack from Leston for the entire distance. Despite being handicapped by a broken anti-roll bar bracket, which manifestly upset the car's handling on right-handers, Warner refused to yield despite the occasional friendly nudge from his rival. Gregor Grant enthused in *Autosport*: "Warner and Leston continued their duel right up to the finishing line, the former getting home [first] by 5/8 of a second."

With the team's confidence at its highest all year, the 'Flag made for Snetterton, and the longest Formula Junior race on the national calendar: the Eastern Counties 100 Trophy on June 18. With Parkes unavailable for the 100-mile event, Warner joined Moss in the sister Gemini. The team chief, enjoying his first single-seater start of the year, promptly upset the form book by lapping below the lap record in practice, with Moss also qualifying on the second row. Unfortunately, Warner inadvertently selected fourth gear rather than first as the flag dropped, which resulted in his black and white Gemini being engulfed by the pack. Undeterred, he then put on a comeback charge – at the end of the first lap he was running in eighteenth place. Three tours later he was lying tenth, taking another position the next time around. At half-distance into the 37-lap race, he was up with the leading bunch which comprised Alan Rees, Peter Arundell, Moss, Peter Warr and Mike McKee. Positions remained largely static until Moss' Gemini retired at the Esses with just three laps remaining after it ran a bearing, Warner having by now vaulted to fourth place. He would eventually place third overall behind Lotus 20 duo Arundell and Rees. Unfortunately, luck deserted him in the GT race after a rear shock absorber seized in the middle of the

Parkes is seen here leading eventual winner Moss at Brands Hatch in June 1960, where the works Gemini-Fords took a resounding one-two finish in The John Davy Trophy Formula Junior race.

Esses, which pitched LOV1 off the circuit and allowed arch-rival Leston to assume the lead.

Then came the team's first overseas foray of the year, the Coupe International de Vitesse des Formule Junior encounter at Rheims on July 2, which was a support race for the French Grand Prix. Team Lotus laid down a marker early on, Trevor Taylor's car featuring a 1.1-litre Cosworth-Ford engine, along with 6.5in by 15in rear tyres. The Yorkshireman scorched to a practice time of 2min 46.4sec, comfortably the fastest of all three timed sessions. Only eight of the 40 or so runners managed to get below the 2min 50sec barrier. Warner recalls: "New regulations allowed bigger engines with only a slight weight penalty. Colin Chapman persuaded Cosworth not to supply these units to rival teams, so the Lotuses were always going to be tough to beat."

Parkes arrived at the circuit on the Friday before the race, having missed the first two practice sessions. He showcased his customary adaptability by clocking a time of 2min 49sec inside his first 15 laps of the circuit, despite a lack of familiarity with the venue. With the race being run over three heats, the victor decided on aggregate, it was Taylor's Lotus 20 which predictably headed home the Cooper of Tony Maggs in the opener, with Moss third in the other works Gemini. Parkes' good work, however, was undone after he missed a gear accelerating out of the Muizon hairpin. The clutch exploded, showering shrapnel across the track and ending his day prematurely. In the second heat, Maggs led home Taylor, with Dick Prior third ahead of Moss.

The final heat was held following the Grand Prix, in which Ferrari's Giancarlo Baghetti caused arguably the greatest upset win in Formula One history by winning on his World Championship debut. It was now past 5pm, the two prior Formula Junior races and 52 laps of the banner event having left the track surface a greasy

Bill Moss' Gemini ducks inside the Tyrrell-Cooper of John Love en route to fourth place in the first heat of the British Empire Trophy support race at Silverstone in June 1961.

oil-coated mess. On the first lap, there were several spinners at the Thillois hairpin, Moss among them. Nonetheless, he returned trackside in sixth place only to perform another pirouette on the fourth lap. This time, his off-piste excursion was permanent: the Gemini glanced off a bank, damaging the rear glassfibre body section, a radius arm and a gearlever rod. Including practice, Moss had to that point covered 285 miles and, with only another 24 miles left to run, he was forced to rue the passing of a likely third place finish on aggregate. It was left to Taylor to take home the spoils ahead of Maggs and Swiss up-and-comer Jo Siffert.

The two Geminis were back in Chiswick by the following Wednesday. This gave the team's hard-pressed mechanics little time to repair them for the British Empire Trophy meeting at Silverstone the following weekend. Nonetheless, both cars made it to Northamptonshire, the oversubscribed entry leading the BRDC to instigate two races with the overall winner being decided on aggregate. The Team Lotus cars were equipped with the larger displacement 1.1-litre engines and, as such, were going to be tough to beat, with Trevor Taylor leading home Peter Arundell for a Lotus one-two. Bill Moss' entry was the first Gemini home in seventh place over the combined distance, with team-mate Parkes down in ninth.

Competing in the GT race at the same meeting, Warner's practice run was curtailed by a worrying drop in oil pressure which was later traced to a faulty relief valve. The Warner-Leston rivalry picked up from where it left off come the race, the former's superior start seeing him fend off his adversary for 15 laps, only to lose his advantage at Copse corner after an errant backmarker tripped him up. The ensuing spin cost him the class lead and he was nine seconds down on his nemesis on returning trackside. With five laps to go, the gap stood at five seconds and closing, Leston's Elite having by now developed an electrical glitch which would soon halt it. Warner assumed control and was set for more silverware, only for the engine to let go in the biggest way possible as they passed the pits for the final time.

Unbowed, Warner and the newly re-engined Elite were at Snetterton for the July 23 Archie Scott Brown meeting, with the works Geminis being entered in both the Formula Junior and Formula Libre races. Parkes was set for a packed itinerary, the lofty all-rounder also tackling the main GT race and the saloon car race. It was Warner, however, who slackened jaws with his performance in practice for the Scott Brown Memorial Trophy headliner. He circulated in 1min 48.7sec, quicker than the other runners, bar the 3.8-litre

Jaguar E-types of Parkes and Roy Salvadori. After making light work of the *Autosport* Class B opener, he was on equally imperious form in the Archie Scott Brown feature. While the race was won outright by Parkes, who fended off Salvadori from start to finish, Warner and LOV1 overcame a significant horsepower disadvantage to place ahead of all the other Jaguar runners to finish a fine third overall, and class victor.

Moss, meanwhile, was all over Dick Prior's larger capacity Lola in the early stages of the oversubscribed Formula Junior race, with Parkes holding down fourth place behind Brian Whitehouse in George Henrotte's Lotus. This became third place after the clutch in Moss' Mk3A detonated before half distance. Parkes then jumped Whitehouse on the eighth lap and gained on Prior, but ultimately had to settle for the runner-up spot. He was then instructed, as *Autosport* put it, to "... rush off and beat up the F2 Coopers, various sports cars and Keith Greene's F1 Gilby" in the 15-lap Formula Libre finale. He did as he was told, and became embroiled in a ding-dong slipstreaming battle with Greene's Grand Prix weapon. Despite the inequality between cars – pushrod Ford versus purebred Coventry Climax FPF power – Parkes maintained second place for four laps, only for a stone to pierce the Gemini's radiator, which ended play.

On to Brands Hatch for the August Bank Holiday Guards Trophy meeting. Warner anticipated rain and made the best possible use of the latest German SP wet-weather tyres in practice for the Peco Trophy race. He lapped a clear two seconds faster than anyone else, including Parkes, who was armed with an Equipe Endeavour Ferrari. Inclement weather would undoubtedly have favoured small-capacity cars, rain being a great equaliser. However, the sun emerged in time for the race, and with it the chance of a shock outright win all but evaporated. Nonetheless, as Stirling Moss ran out the overall winner aboard his Rob Walker Ferrari, Warner and Leston slugged it out for class honours. LOV1 was in front – barely – until a grassy moment with just seven laps left to run allowed DAD10 past. Warner soon closed in on his arch-rival, only to lose out while negotiating traffic.

The 'Flag would also emerge without a win in the Formula Junior support race, but it would not be for the want of trying. Trevor Taylor led the way at the start, only for the car's gearlever to come adrift by the time he arrived at the first corner. Parkes, meanwhile, was forced to take to the grass in avoidance of the ailing Lotus 20 which bundled him down the order. With Cooper pilot Tony Maggs having assumed the lead, further chaos ensued after his team-mate, John Love, spun going past the back of the pits, which in turn slowed the rest of the field. This enabled Maggs to make a break for it, the Rhodesian establishing a seemingly unassailable lead, with Team Lotus man Peter Arundell holding down second place as a recovering Parkes climbed from ninth to third in the works Gemini. Both clawed back the deficit to Maggs and passed him on the eleventh tour. Moss, meanwhile, was lying fourth in the sister Mk3A. His position appeared secure until the clutch began slipping. He then became easy pickings for Lola man Peter Ashdown and the recovering Love but managed to cling on for sixth place at the flag. Parkes, meanwhile, was unable to overcome the 100cc disparity between his Gemini and Arundell's Lotus and finished a mere tenth of a second behind the winner, with both future Grand Prix pilots sharing the fastest lap.

Next up was the prestigious Goodwood TT meeting on August 20. Uniquely, the length of the Tourist Trophy race for GT cars was such that drivers could not also compete in the BARC Formula Junior support races – much to the annoyance of Mike Parkes. With the lead Gemini seat now open, Bill McCowen was re-enlisted on a one-off basis. Warner, meanwhile, was keen to inflict a major upset in the 100-mile main event.

"We had a chance of international glory in the Tourist Trophy race. Hopes were high for LOV1 as we knew the tyres would last the distance, and we fitted a larger fuel tank and an extra oil tank so that we could do the whole race without a pit stop. The Ferraris and the Aston Martins, we reasoned, would need four or five stops for fuel and tyres. We even practiced pit stops to fool the opposition, making it look very dramatic by deliberately coming in too fast for a change of tyres ... perhaps a bit too fast as I was hauled in front of the stewards! We knew from talking with Keith Duckworth, who'd built the engine, that so long as we kept the revs down we could do the race nonstop and still be quick. We set a target time, and in the race I consistently lapped below it. I was going relatively gently when a wheel bearing failed half an hour in. Stirling Moss won in Rob Walker's Ferrari, famously listening to Raymond Baxter's commentary of the race on the car's radio. Ours was a never-to-be-repeated opportunity to win a major event, one with an illustrious history. It was hugely disappointing."

Earlier in the day, Bill Moss had upheld Gemini honour in the BARC Formula Junior curtain raiser, setting the race's fastest lap en route to third place behind Frank Gardner's Lotus-Ford and John Rhodes in the Midlands Racing Partnership Cooper-BMC. Matters didn't run quite so smoothly for the team in the second instalment, which was won by Team Lotus man Alan Rees from Dick Prior and Dennis Taylor. While unable to make inroads on the lead trio, McCowen appeared destined for fourth place despite the close attention of Lotus drivers Jon Leighton and Angus Hyslop. However, his good work was undone on the final tour when, as *Autosport* put it, he "... went 'wattle fencing' coming out of the chicane and spun off into the bank, filling the exhaust with good Sussex earth which prevented him from starting up again ... he had to retire only 30 or 40 yards from the flag."

In the final, Moss left the line first but came home a dispirited fifth.

Throughout the season, the factory Geminis had been competing in two series: the Motor Racing Championship and the BRSCC John Davy Trophy. Having concentrated primarily on the main category, with only involvement in latter, Warner was surprised to learn at this juncture that both of his drivers were likely candidates for the Trophy prize. This prompted the decision not to sit out the August 27 round at Brands Hatch, the 'Flag drivers scraping in as reserves. It was a wise decision, as on making the cut due to no-shows, both of his drivers blitzed their way to pole slots in their respective heats. Parkes and Moss then claimed a victory apiece, with Parkes prevailing in the final over his team-mate. As well as a morale boost, these results further consolidated their Trophy standings.

September '61 began with hopes of a return visit to The Netherlands for the third instalment of the *Autosport*-backed World Cup meetings, which that year comprised just one event. This time around, however, there was a full German team to take on the Dutch and British squads, with separate prizes for Holland v United Kingdom and Holland v Germany, along with the overall national spoils. On top of that, the programme at the Zandvoort venue also included Formula Junior and Formula Libre contests which attracted the cream of the international talent. Bill Moss was charged with leading the Gemini entries, the sister car being entered for local hero Rob Slotemaker.

As the field tore away in the Formula Junior encounter, the unfortunate Moss was clattered from behind. That spun him around in time for a further battering from the squabbling pack. His Gemini was struck on all four corners and so his race was run, Moss fortunate to have avoided injury. His new team-mate didn't fare much better, Slotemaker getting pinched in a pincer movement at the start. He would make it as far as the second corner – a fast right-hander – before tobogganing off the road and into a wire fence.

With the Dutch and German contingent consisting largely of Porsches – and the latest 356B Abarth GTL models at that – the UK troop appeared hopelessly outgunned ahead of the World Cup headliner, with Warner's Elite being joined by Wold Cup returnee Pat Fergusson's Turner-Climax, Tony Lanfranchi's Elva Courier, Tommy Entwhistle's TVR Grantura, and a brace of Marcoses driven by John Mitchell and John Sutton. LOV1 was the sole British challenger that could stay with the quad-cam Porsches – so long as it held together.

After placing second in first practice, the Elite acquired a metallic resonance under acceleration early in the following session. On heading back into the pits, the engine seized solid. The motor was in the process of being removed, only for the circuit's owner to halt proceedings as he point blank refused to let anyone work on site until the doors were opened the following morning at 8am. Fortunately, Dutch racer Ad Bouwmeester rode to the rescue and phoned around various garages until he found one that was prepared to stay open through the night. Team mechanic Geoff Rumble then set about stripping the car's Coventry Climax unit, the cause of the problem being traced to a small ball of aluminium which had jammed the combustion chamber after passing through the intakes of the Weber carbs. Warner recalls: "Wire-mesh protected the trunking which fed the alloy cold-air box, and its lid was located by over-centre fasteners. It clearly hadn't come off the engine, so draw your own conclusions as to how it got there ..."

An exhausted Rumble had the engine in situ the following morning, barely ten minutes before the 50 lap race was due to begin. What followed next was arguably Warner's finest hour as a driver. At the start, it was the Porsche-Abarths of local ace Ben Pon and German Fritz Hahnl which set the pace, with Gerhard Koch in third someway clear of Warner, who had Fergusson's Turner in close proximity. Rules dictated that each driver had to make a compulsory pit stop to take on a gallon of fuel supplied by the organisers in a

Right: LOV1 blasts-off the line alongside Graham Hill's Jaguar, Mike Parkes' Ferrari, and Roy Salvadori's E-type at the start of the July 1961 Archie Scott Brown Memorial Trophy GT race. Warner would emerge a remarkable third overall, and first in class.

TAKE COURAGE
BP SUPER PLUS
109
108

PLAYER'S
DUNLOP
SUPER-PLUS
CHAMPION
CASTROL
LUCAS
CARSAVERS PLAN
ENERGOL
THE MOTOR
BP ENERGOL MOTOR OIL
BP SUPER PLUS
LUCAS

sealed container. Prior to the race, Warner concluded that it would be best to get this over and done with early on and so become faster towards the end of the race on a lighter fuel load. And so on the eleventh lap, by which time it was up to third place, LOV1 shot into the pits to take on petrol before returning trackside a full minute down on the warring leaders.

Against expectations, this grew to 65sec inside a further four laps but Pon and Hahnl had yet to stop. While apparently safe in third place, the deficit to the Porsche duo seemed insurmountable with the gap standing at 67sec with 26 laps left to run. However, the Sisyphean task suddenly became a lot easier after Hahnl pitted two tours later. Once back on track he promptly spun, which allowed Warner to close to within 11 seconds of him. Two laps later, Pon made his stop in record time and emerged 33 seconds ahead of the second place battle. On lap 31, Warner took Hahnl with the leader now 25 seconds ahead. Lapping consistently below the lap record, Warner proceeded to reel-in Pon until, with eight laps left to run, the distance between the lead Porsche and the flying Lotus stood at just four seconds and closing.

The brakes on Pon's car were by now weakened, the Grand Prix occasional struggling to negotiate the second gear hairpin at the end of the pit straight. The Dutchman was forced to brake earlier and earlier, a point not lost on Warner, who out-braked him at this very spot with four laps remaining, only for Pon to retake the position at the next corner. On the next tour, Pon hoved into view on the pit straight with Warner glued to his tail. He promptly pulled out of the Porsche's slipstream to assume the lead which he wouldn't relinquish, his fastest lap of 1min 49.9sec being the quickest ever for a GT car at Zandvoort. To crown his solo performance, the entire British contingent completed the distance to rack up a total of 39 points, which comfortably beat the depleted Dutch and German teams with 29 and 28 points respectively.

Following assorted logistical problems, the transporter didn't arrive back in Chiswick for a further ten days, which meant time was pressing prior to the next meeting, the prestigious International Gold Cup meeting at Oulton Park on September 23, with Moss' car in particular requiring extensive repairs. Unfortunately, the mechanics' burning of midnight oil was for nought. After lapping below the existing

Warner chases down Ben Pon's Porsche-Abarth to take a brilliant win in the *Autosport* World Cup race at Zandvoort.

Formula Junior lap record in practice at the Cheshire venue, Moss was taken out by the Lotus, driven by the abnormally brave Jack Pearce. The newly rebuilt Gemini was a write-off. The sister car, now also equipped with a 1.1-litre engine and driven by returnee Parkes, was quick to leave the front row at the start of the race only to be stripped of third gear early on in proceedings. Parkes would place a lowly sixth, the race being won in masterful style by Tony Maggs.

With the Geminis and LOV1 entered for the following weekend's meeting at Snetterton, the team was faced with the trifling matter of building a new Mk3A from scratch, repairing the gearbox in Parkes' car, and delivering both engines to Cosworth for rebuilds. Incredibly they did just that, Parkes rewarding their efforts with pole for the Vanwall Trophy Formula Junior encounter, Moss lining-up behind him on the grid. While the boss' outing in the Molyslip Trophy race ended after the differential worked its way loose, the Gemini duo excelled, with Parkes leading from the third lap to the flag, and Moss jumping early leader Maggs in the closing stages for second place. The cars were then immediately loaded into the transporter for the John Davy Trophy round at Brands Hatch the following day.

With Parkes and Moss both starting from the front row for the 20-lap race over the full Grand Prix circuit, the Geminis, along with the Lotus of Dennis Taylor, scorched clear of the pack at the start. Moss was soon forced to retire after a stone holed his car's radiator,

but Parkes bested a determined Taylor to triumph by five seconds. Despite his failure to finish, Moss' lead in the championship standings was conclusive, and he was crowned the 1961 champion.

The Brands Hatch outing also signalled the end of Parkes' campaign with the 'Flag. The season was by now drawing rapidly to a close, the penultimate meeting of the year proving one of the squad's most fulfilling. Armed with a MK3A destined for an overseas buyer, Moss was entered in the Formula Junior and Formula Libre races at Silverstone on October 1. Warner, meanwhile, was back in harness for the GT race, and purely for a laugh he also signed on for the Unlimited Sports Car contest. Having been a late entrant for the latter event, he was obliged to start from the final slot on the ninth row of the grid. By quarter distance he was in fifth place, harrying the John Bekaert's Lola and Mike Beckwith's Lotus ahead. He failed to move further up the order but battled all the way to the line, finishing barely half a car's length behind Beckwith's sports-racer. In the GT race, he assumed the lead on the second lap and headed home assorted Jaguar E-types and David Hobbs' Elite by 25 seconds. Warner explains: "A brake union broke which caused the brakes to fail completely with two laps to go, which reduced my lap times considerably!"

Moss continued where Warner had left off aboard his red customer car, winning both single-seater races at a canter. The 'Flag left Kent with three wins and as many fastest laps from four starts. It would have been a near perfect season finale, but Moss had been entered in the BRSCC Formula Junior race at Snetterton on October 7. After qualifying on pole, he was comfortably leading, only to retire with brake failure which allowed Frank Gardner through to win aboard Jim Russell's Lotus 20.

Despite more than a few heartaches, sleepless nights and costly mishaps, The Chequered Flag équipe had overcome a poor start to rack up the silverware in '61. Life for Graham Warner, however, was about to become even busier.

Mike Parkes returned to the 'Flag team for the September 1961 Formula Junior race. He claimed outright honours in his works Gemini Mk3A, and is seen here receiving the Vanwall Trophy.

VI. Blazing trails

Following a largely rewarding season of motorsport in 1961, hopes were high ahead of the 1962 season. Warner in particular was keen to progress as a driver, but also as a constructor. Having taken the fight to the hitherto dominant Lotus 20s with the Gemini Mk3, the next generation of single-seater to emerge from the 'Flag would be several steps removed from the norm in a bid to stay ahead. Designed by Warner, Roy Thomas and Geoff Rumble, this brave new design was daring both in specification and appearance. However, as the team was about to discover, blazing trails is an easy way to get burned.

For Warner, 1962 would prove a pivotal year both as a driver and as a racing car manufacturer. "The Mk4 was designed and manufactured in-house. My aim was to produce sufficient improvement on the successful Mk3 to keep ahead of Lotus, Cooper, Lola and Brabham for the next two seasons, and also be competitive in other disciplines with suitable engines, should we decide to look elsewhere. The frontal area was reduced to a minimum, and the chassis was four inches narrower than the outgoing car. The driving position was semi-reclined, the engine was lowered and canted over – both engine and gearbox were designed for dry-sump lubrication – but this was not adopted due to the extra cost. These measures, along with the low-mounted pannier fuel tanks, lowered the centre of gravity.

"We paid serious attention to the aerodynamics, too: the body was designed to offer minimal resistance to airflow, and to this end it had carefully ducted side-mounted radiators and a 'bullet' nose. The front suspension was inboard; it had 9.5in disc brakes and much lighter magnesium wheels and hubs. This permitted the use of softer springs and better-controlled suspension damping. The use of inboard brakes also meant an increase in wheelbase, so the track was widened to keep the ratio between the two the same as on the Mk3A. This also decreased drag from the airflow between the body and the wheels. To further aid the airflow, the front hubs, steering arms, ball joints, outer U/Js, etc, were recessed within the deeply-dished 13in wheels; the trackrod and anti-roll bar were aligned with the wishbones. After the prototype had been built, the steel upper front wishbones, which pivoted on roller bearings, were streamlined. The oil cooler was also moved from behind the seat to beneath the nose as it didn't receive enough air in its original position."

Autosport trumpeted the arrival of the car in January '62, stating: "There is a possibility of a rear-engined sports car being developed from this very advanced machine."

According to Warner this was never on the cards: "My thoughts were that if we wanted to step into Formula Two or suchlike, we had a good foundation in the Mk4. As for a sports car, the closest we came was when Ford was looking for a partner to build the GT40 sports-prototype. It had tried to buy Ferrari, and Enzo Ferrari famously showed Henry Ford II the door when a deal was close. Ford then sought out British design know-how in order to build a Le Mans car with which to beat the Italians. A delegation was sent to Lotus, Cooper, Lola, and us. When the people came over from Detroit and saw our facilities they were horrified! That said, Eric Broadley at Lola got the job and his place in Bromley wasn't much better."

Having sold his Elite at the end of the previous year, it was a case of onwards and upwards for Warner trackside – in theory. "Colin Chapman once told me that the results we achieved with LOV1 helped him sell more Elites than any other rival Lotus racer – it was

And left: The new Gemini Mk4 was as daring as Formula Junior design got in 1962. Designed by Graham Warner, Roy Thomas and Geoff Rumble.

a great advert for the model. Whether he was just bullshitting because he wanted something, I don't know, but I believed him. However, I knew it was time to move on. I had a chance of a semi-works Jaguar drive with John Coombs' team, racing a Mk2 saloon and an E-type, but he was aligned with Shell and BP. Mike Parkes also tried to get me in with Ecurie Endeavour, but it was the same story. Geoff Murdoch, who was the competitions manager at Esso with whom I was tied, then suggested Aston Martin. I was informed that the factory was going to be involved in running cars at arm's length via John Ogier. He had originally run a DBR1 and DB4GT, but more recently had entered a pair of lightweight Zagato-bodied DB4s registered 1VEV and 2VEV. I went for a test at Goodwood and got down to Roy Salvadori's time in the same car on the same fuel load and tyres, and then had a go in the older DBR1 sports-racer. I was then offered the drive."

Aston Martin had officially withdrawn from motorsport after winning the 1959 World Sports Car Championship, but the Newport Pagnell concern still supported privateer teams. Ogier, a wealthy poultry farmer, received more support than most: his Essex Racing Stable équipe operated out of his East Hanningfield farm near Chelmsford, where three mechanics formed the core of the staff under the management of Eric Hind. Having landed one drive, Warner then batted away another after being sounded out about a possible seat with the works Cooper squad. "I went so far as taking part in a test day at Brands Hatch where I drove an F2 car but I didn't like it at all. There was talk of a Formula One drive of some

sort but I felt I was not ready for such a big jump at that time and declined the offer. In retrospect, I think I made the right decision. In May of that year I also had the opportunity to do the Nürburgring 1000km alongside Bruce McLaren in Ogier's DBR1, which I also turned down. Trying to learn a circuit as daunting as that and make the leap from a 1220cc GT car to an out-and-out sports-racer was too much, so I suggested Tony Maggs for the drive and he got it."

The 'Flag's race programme was due to kick-off at the SMRC meeting at Snetterton on March 23, with Bill Moss being retained for a second season. The other seat was to be filled by cycling-star-turned-rally ace, Peter Proctor. Proctor had also shown form in Formula Junior aboard a Lotus 18 and an Alexis Mk3. With neither works Gemini completed in time for the Snetterton round, Moss dusted off his old Lotus 18 while the boss stayed in Chiswick. This was for the best; otherwise he would have seen his much-loved former mount destroyed in a horrific shunt at the same meeting. The Elite had been acquired by Dick Gibson, who had regularly battled with Warner in '61 aboard his hot-rodded Jaguar XK120. In only his second outing in the diminutive Lotus, Gibson was in pursuit of two Jaguar E-types, only to put a rear wheel on the grass. He then slewed across the track before flipping the car and reducing it to its constituent parts against the bank opposite. If it appeared that Gibson's predicament couldn't get any worse, the engine and gearbox – the few parts of the car that remained intact following the crash – were stolen from the filling station on the back straight where the wreck was being stored while he was convalescing in hospital.

And left: Graham Warner sold LOV to Dick Gibson for the 1962 season. Unfortunately, the car was written-off at Snetterton in March 1962. The car's Coventry Climax engine was stolen while he was recuperating in hospital.

Bill Moss attempts to stay dry ahead of the May 1962 Formula Junior race at Silverstone, from which he would retire his factory Gemini Mk4.

Cycling star turned race and rally driver Peter Proctor before the start of the sodden Formula Junior race at the *Daily Express* International Trophy Formula Junior race at Silverstone. He would finish fifth in his Gemini Mk4.

The Gemini Mk4 debuted at Goodwood on April 23, with only one car having been completed in time: Moss retired the prototype on the third lap of the BARC Formula Junior encounter with an overheating engine. Proctor then took over for the Aintree 200 meeting the following weekend, only to drop out on discovering a 'box full of neutrals'. With both works cars on hand for the wet *Daily Express* International Trophy meeting at Silverstone on May 12 hopes of recording a maiden finish were achieved with Proctor's fine fifth place on the waterlogged circuit. He had Mike Spence's Lotus 22 and Richard Attwood's Cooper T59 in close proximity behind him for much of the running, and he

Bill Moss chases down John Love's Cooper at Crystal Palace in June 1962. He would finish fifth in the Formula Junior race in his works Gemini Mk4.

was catching John Rhodes' ailing Ausper T4 in the dying stages. His team-mate, meanwhile, failed to finish after his car died unexpectedly at Abbey Curve.

Matters seemed to take a turn for the better during the May 27 BRSCC meeting at Brands Hatch. Moss assumed the lead inside a couple of laps, with Proctor holding down third place, but both cars were out before half-distance with fractured brake caliper cross-over pipes. With the Mk4 still some way short of being sorted, plans to enter the Monaco Grand Prix support race that month were abandoned, with Proctor accepting a drive in Ken Tyrrell's Cooper instead. He was back in a Gemini for the BARC Anerley Trophy race at Crystal Palace on June 11, only to scratch his entry following a gearbox breakage in qualifying. Moss, meanwhile, finished behind Denny Hulme's Brabham BT2 in fifth place. Then disaster struck. Both Geminis were entered in the Coupe International de Vitesse des Juniors race at the Reims-Gueux circuit in on June 1, only for the team to discover a stability issue under full throttle on the long, high-speed circuit. Improvements were made, but even Moss at his bravest was still three seconds slower than Peter Arundell in the works Lotus 22 around the 4.8 mile lap. Tragically, the opening heat saw Moss and 22-year-old American-born Canadian Peter Ryan collide at the extremely fast curve after the pit straight. The latter was thrown clear of his car, and ultimately succumbed to internal injuries. Moss, meanwhile, remained in his car and had to be freed. Miraculously, the worst injury he incurred was a cut to his face. Proctor participated in the second heat but freely admitted in his autobiography, *Pedals and Pistons*, that "… my heart was not in my race."

Warner, meanwhile, was at a low ebb. "Bill survived, thank God, with severe bruising to his shoulders from the upper chassis tubes, which he told me kept him in the car, unlike poor Ryan, and that saved his life. The chassis tubes didn't carry coolant – as was the case with many rival designs – so he also avoided being scalded when some of the pipes fractured. Also, the pannier fuel tanks didn't leak, whereas in cars such as the Lotus 18, the fuel tank was situated over the driver's knees. As a team, we were really starting to suffer, though. We had put so much effort into the car – and considerable expenditure – but without meaningful results there was no prize money being generated. By that point in the season it was becoming increasingly hard to stay motivated."

Warner's own driving ambitions had got off to a shaky start at Goodwood for the Easter meeting on April 23, as he pirouetted the Aston 1VEV at Lavant on the opening lap of the 15-lap Sussex Trophy race. While Innes Ireland romped into the distance to win aboard his Lotus 19-Climax, Warner recovered to take seventh place, taking 0.2 seconds off Roy Salvadori's '61 lap record in the same car and on the same tyres by way of consolation. His next outing would be in a Gemini at Rouen-Les-Essarts which supported the July 8 French Grand Prix. Standing in for the injured Moss while Proctor sat out the meeting, he would finish 19th in the first heat and 12th in the second after gear-selection problems.

A month passed before the 'Flag's next appearance at the August 6 BRSCC Championship round at Brands Hatch, with the single car of Proctor classified as finishing in ninth place. Days later he was offered a full-time drive with Ken Tyrrell for the following year which the modest Yorkshireman accepted. He would make only one more appearance in a Gemini, being joined by hillclimb ace Tony Marsh in the sister car for the September 29 BARC Vanwall Trophy meeting at Snetterton. Both cars retired. Ironically, that same day witnessed the sole win for a Mk4 that season, with privateer John Pollock edging out Lotus 22 driver Malcolm Templeton in a thinly-supported Formula Junior thrash at Kirkistown, Northern Ireland.

"We didn't have the financial clout to develop what was an innovative design," Warner recalls. "The car's Achilles' Heel was its six-speed gearbox. At that time it was unprecedented in the racing world – let along the production car arena – to have six speeds. Most cars made do with four. We had to use a production car casing, and the one we borrowed from the Renault Dauphine was insufficiently rigid, although we doubled the depth of the special alloy plate which bolted to the top [this housed the gear change mechanism] to stiffen it, but this didn't eliminate flexing under load. The cramming of the narrow, straight-cut gears into the small casing also caused many gearbox failures. The cars were too far ahead of their time to be run by a small team with limited resources."

Warner's own trackside engagements had become increasingly sporadic as work interrupted play. His second outing for Ogier's équipe was as team-mate to Jim Clark at the August 24 Tourist Trophy meeting at Goodwood. "I managed only a few laps of the TT. The car hadn't been well in the run up to the race and sounded awful at the start. I pitted, the mechanics changed a couple of plugs, but it still wouldn't run on all six-cylinders, so the car was retired. To be honest, the Astons were outclassed by purpose-built

73

A pensive-looking Graham Warner (in helmet) prior to the start of the August 1962 Tourist Trophy race at Goodwood.

racing cars as opposed to modified road cars. Most unusually, we found that the Zagatos were quicker with full fuel tanks. Although heavier, the better weight distribution improved handling, and the slightly raised nose helped top speed."

With the core car sales business impeded by hire purchase restrictions intended to reduce demand, something had to give. The Gemini marque was quietly axed, with George Henrotte taking over the team cars, but there would be one final hurrah that season. A new star shone vividly during the BRSCC Boxing day at Brands Hatch round 18 of the John Davy Trophy series.

American driver Roy Pike had driven his prior mount, an Ausper T3, with great verve that season, and the Kent showing was his maiden outing aboard the Mk4 following a test at Goodwood. As expected, Denny Hulme had laid down a marker in practice: armed with a works Brabham BT2, complete with five-bearing Holbay-Ford engine, he lapped more than a second below the existing lap record. His likeliest challenger appeared to be John Fenning, who was having his final run with Ron Harris' Lola team. But, as *Autosport* reported, it was Pike who initially made hay come race day: "Hulme made a poor start and it was a white streak that detached itself from the grid to lead into Paddock bend – it was Roy Pike's Gemini … Hulme eventually achieved second place on the second lap and he was right on Pike's heels, the Gemini emitting alarming quantities of smoke when emerging from corners, but continuing nonetheless."

The Californian, who was tended to that day by 'Flag alumnus Roy Thomas, recalls: "Unfortunately Tom the Weld overfilled the engine with oil, hence the smoke. Hulme eventually got past me at Druids, and then Fenning, who I then had off at Clearways. It was the first time I'd ever touched anyone in a motor race." The result was instant retirement for both drivers, but if nothing else Pike had put himself on Graham Warner's radar and would in time become a 'Flag regular.

Heading into 1963, the team's programme was centred on the new Lotus Elan, the latest sports car to emerge from the Norfolk marque. The firm's company principal Colin Chapman was too busy pushing envelopes and breaking moulds to factor in the whole profit-making aspect. The Elan was a lesson in simplicity by comparison: initially conceived as a low-cost replacement for the altogether more basic Seven, the kernel of the Elan as a more aspirational product took root once it became clear that the Elite would likely bankrupt Lotus. Its design was influenced as much by bottom-line-minded prudence as starry-eyed futurism, the use of a steel backbone chassis becoming a marque constant for generations to come. Easy to fabricate, and weighing a mere 75lb, it measured just 11.5in by 6in at its centre. Suspension was by tubular steel wishbones with coil springs/dampers up front, to the rear a wide-based lower wishbone and coil/spring damper unit arrangement. The lower end of the strut was fixed in a cast ally housing which contained the wheel bearing and hubs, in addition to lugs for mounting the disc brakes (inboard at the rear).

Then there was the powerplant. A classic of its kind, the Elan's twin-cam unit was conceived by Harry Mundy. The former BRM and Coventry Climax man rustled up an alloy cylinder head for the Ford 116E five-bearing block and the resultant four displaced 1499cc. It was essentially a de-tuned version of the same engine which had made such an impact when powering Jim Clark's headline-making Lotus 23 at

Warner steers John Ogier's Aston Martin DB4GT Zagato through the chicane at Goodwood, en route to seventh place in the 1962 Sussex Trophy race.

that year's Nürburgring 1000km race. But after the first 22 cars had been made (all of them subsequently recalled), capacity was increased to 1558cc with Cosworth's Keith Duckworth lending a fettling hand.

Clothing all this was a pretty glassfibre body shaped by former Ford man Ron Hickman. Offered in kit form at £1095, or fully-built for an extra £400, it was an instant hit, even if build quality was, at best, inconsistent. Future iterations would rectify this, all things being relative, but a racing version would have to wait a while, as Warner recalls: "When the car was introduced, even the brochure said it was 'not intended for competition use,' and Chapman discouraged talk of the Elan being raced. I said to him, 'Colin, it's a Lotus. Whether you like it or not, there are people out there who will race it'. He reluctantly came around to the idea and I was tasked with debuting the Elan on a circuit."

Though widely praised for its dexterity on challenging back roads, the Elan was criticised in some quarters for its unpredictability trackside. Testers voiced concerns over its tendency to flex, and suddenly oversteer. They also complained of excessive bumptseer. "The standard Elan wasn't a good track car until we started modifying it," Warner recalls. "I gave the Elan its motorsport baptism at the [May 11 '63] *Express* International meeting at Silverstone and I was not impressed! Our car was standard other than having a Cosworth exhaust, DS11 brake pads, and Dunlop racing tyres. It also proved quicker with the hood in place."

Impressed or not, Warner lay a remarkable fifth overall after three laps, sandwiched between Dick Protheroe's Jaguar E-type and Peter Jopp's AC Cobra. As Graham Hill emerged victorious in John Coombs' 'Lightweight' Jaguar E-type following 25 frenetic racing laps, Warner's tiny Lotus came home an embattled eighth overall. "As the race unfolded, the Elan became more and more unstable under braking. It was 80 per cent there but the backbone chassis would twist, which resulted in violent oversteer. The brakes got progressively worse the more you used them, and there was terrible rear-end steering. After the race we found the rear wishbones had twisted from all the heavy braking. We showed them to Chapman who then put in a little strut between the front and rear wishbone members, immediately inboard of the hub casting, along with a diagonal stiffener which made the whole thing much stronger.

"The car was progressively modified for racing over the course of the season: weight was saved and the suspension was stiffened and lowered with new rose-jointed adjustable wishbones, the diff being raised to suit. We also added Armstrong adjustable dampers, a heavier anti-roll bar, a new adjustable pedal box to suit dual front and rear brake circuits, plus a close-ratio 'box and roller-splined halfshafts to replace the rubber doughnuts which kept failing. Chapman forbade altering the profile of the rear wings so the wishbones were shortened to provide clearance for the wider alloy wheels. An alloy radiator was fitted, and the steering rack mountings strengthened after they had failed as I'd entered the Abbey Corner left-hander during a test at Silverstone – and back then it was virtually flat out!

"On top of all that, we then had Cosworth build us a proper engine which produced around 150bhp. It had an oil-cooler and fresh air box for the twin Weber carburettors. Later on, we also fitted an oil cooler for the diff. The retractable headlights were also changed for fixed items behind Perspex fairings."

These modifications, and those of rival squad Ian Walker Racing, were subsequently adopted for the official 26R competition Elan. "I often hear that IWR

Graham Warner debuted the Lotus Elan in competition during the May 1963 *Express* International meeting at Silverstone. He wasn't impressed …

was responsible for coming up with the 26R but that wasn't the case. As the year went on, Lotus and the 'Flag received more and more enquiries about a full-blown racing version of the Elan, so Chapman decided that Lotus Components would market a proper 'R' for racing version of the Elan – which was known internally as Type 26 – at a higher price. He sent two Team Lotus drivers to test our car at Goodwood: Peter Arundell and Mike Spence, who helped tweak it a bit further. He also agreed that special lighter bodyshells would be made with wider wheelarches to suit the new and much broader centre-lock alloy wheels, and to use alloy castings in the drivetrain which saved more than 120lb. John Miles was then tasked with the homologation and arranging supplies of the special components needed."

Warner and the Elan accrued silverware on only the car's second outing – the Whitsun Trophy race at Goodwood on June 3. As Mike Parkes ran out the winner aboard Maranello Concessionaires' brand new Ferrari 250GTO, Warner broke the lap record for cars with a displacement of up to 2000cc during the wet opening stages en route to a class win and fourth overall following 21 laps of frantic action. With other Elans joining the fray as the year progressed, the second half of the season witnessed greater competition, not least from sometime Gemini pilot John Whitmore in the SMART (Stirling Moss Automobile Racing Team) entry which featured a lightweight 'shell reworked by aerodynamicist Frank Costin.

The friendly rivals next went into battle at the Guards International meeting at Brands Hatch on August 4. Competing in the John Davy Trophy race for sub-2500cc sports cars, there was nothing between them until halfway through the 20-lap thrash, *Autosport* reporting: "Whitmore had the Elan sideways-on in an effort to keep Warner at bay, but the Chequered Flag car passed on Top Straight after 10 laps ... But as Whitmore speeded up in the closing stages, so Warner dropped back with apparent transmission difficulties."

"Actually, it was the clutch; it started slipping," Warner recalls. "I managed to stay ahead of Trevor Taylor's Lotus Elite, though, and also Dickie Stoop's Porsche 356 Carrera." A leaking diff in the Tourist Trophy encounter at Goodwood on August 19 curtailed hopes of further glory.

"By now the SMART car was getting better and better, and at Crystal Palace [on September 7] Whitmore just pipped me to win the Grand Touring race for sub-1600c cars." As *Autosport* reported: "Every time they sped along the start/finish straight, Warner gained a couple of feet, which suggested that the Chequered Flag Elan had a few extra horses over the Stirling Moss-entered one. However, Whitmore, who confessed not to like the circuit, always closed right up elsewhere. Then, on the very last lap, Whitmore actually made it on the inside at Ramp Bend and, with Whitmore right on his tail, he sped into South Tower Corner where the light green Elan was turned so sideways that one wondered if John was going to make a mistake. To an enormous cheer from the spectators, he held it magnificently and beat Graham across the line by three-quarters of a length!"

The same meeting also witnessed George Henrotte's Gemini Mk4 record a long-awaited victory following a largely awful season, Roy Pike gaining pole position and winning the 25-lap BARC London Trophy race for Formula Junior cars from Brian Hart. It would prove the sole win for the model on the British mainland in period. As *Autosport* surmised: "This raised the spirits of this hitherto unlucky equipe no end."

Sadly, it was too little too late for any hopes of a marque revival. The 'Flag's abridged season was effectively over, but not before racer/broadcaster John Bolster got his hands on the Lotus for an *Autosport* track test at Brands Hatch. The veteran journalist commented that, "On the corners, initial understeer could be counterbalanced by applying power, but the most impressive characteristic was the way in which the rear 'hung on.' Eventually, I was daring to use full throttle in corners, which would invite a violent breakaway on a lesser machine. Road holding of this calibre causes the Elan to be very quick out of bends, which is where it often overcomes its rivals ... Apart from the uneven idling, which would not be acceptable in London traffic, this competition car would make an ideal ultra-fast touring machine. To handle it on a racing circuit is to experience very high-performance that can be used to the full all the time." The car was subsequently bought by Hong Kong Lotus agent Arthur Pateman. For 1964, the 'Flag's programme with the Elan was to face fresh opposition. It wouldn't pass without incident.

Overleaf: Warner was pipped to the flag in the September 1963 GT race at Crystal Palace, following an epic battle with John Whitmore's Costin-bodied Elan.

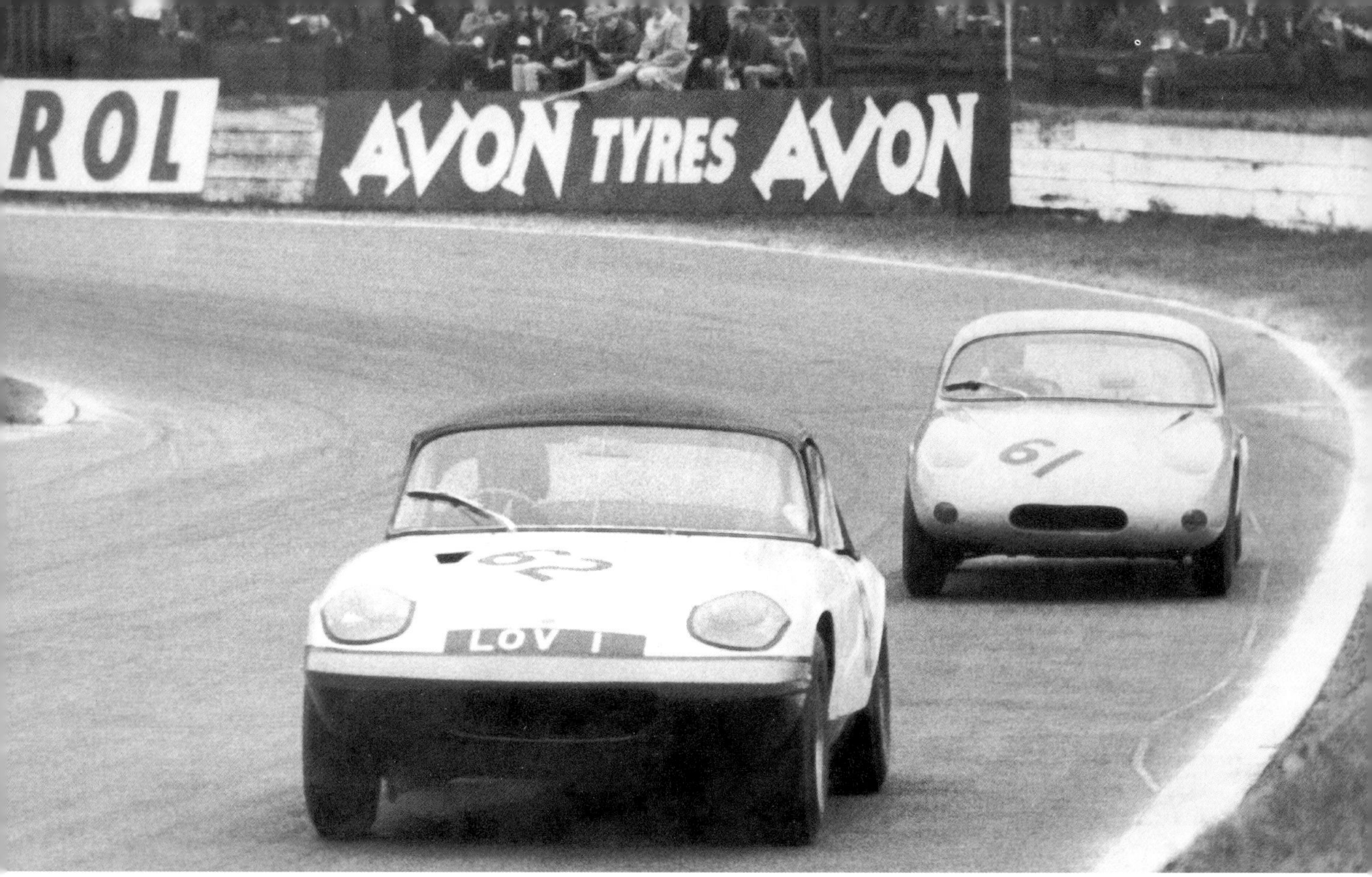
ROL
AVON TYRES AVON
LOV 1

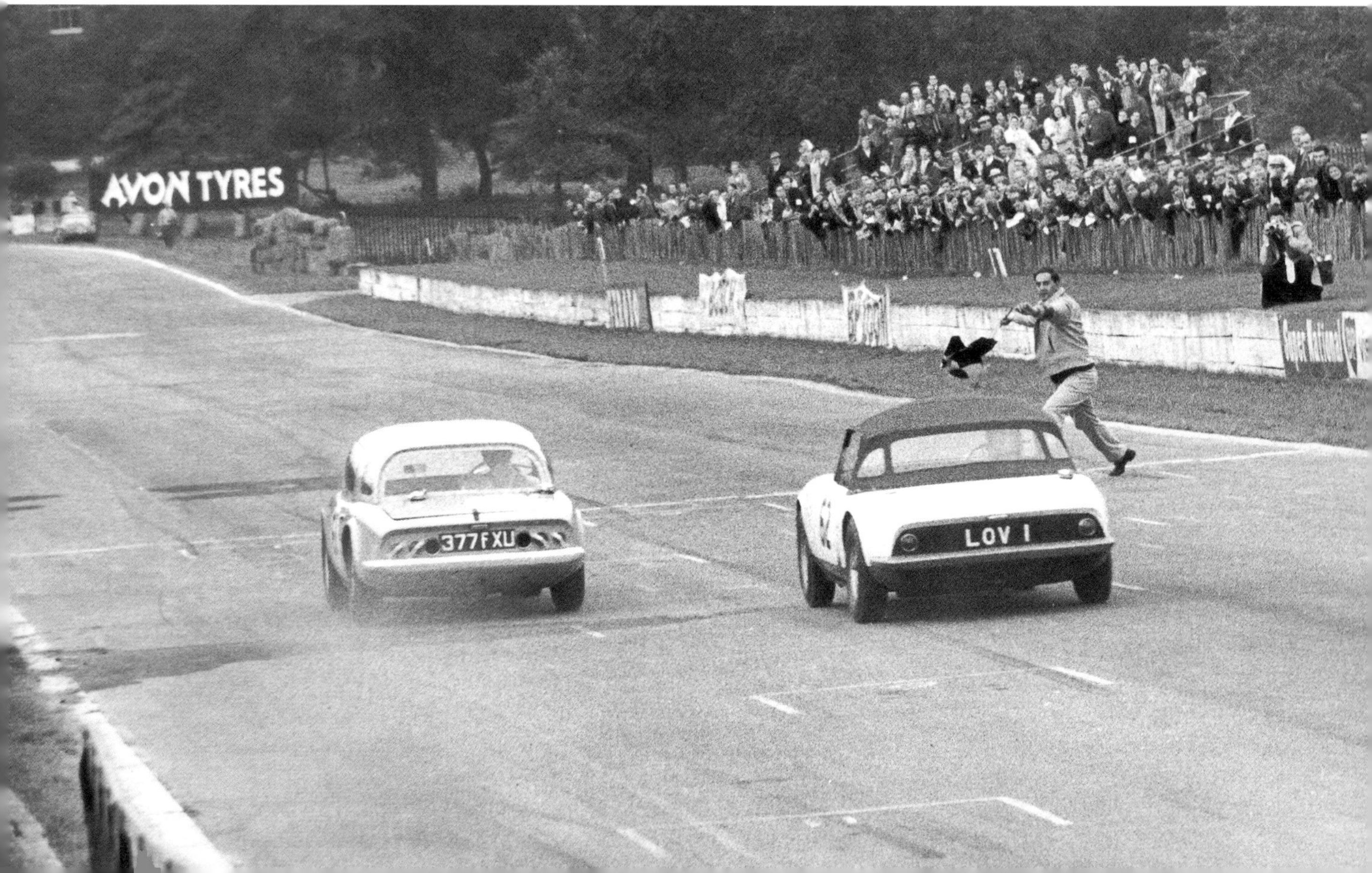
AVON TYRES
377 FXU
LOV 1

VII. Lotus blossoms

Though a declining presence in the single-seater arena, the 'Flag's involvement with the Lotus 26R moved up a gear for '64. Warner recalls: "We received components for the first two cars early that year. It was a bit of a belt-and-braces bid on Lotus' part, with Colin Chapman having arranged with his pal, Ian Walker, to run a pair of cars in addition to us. His team's drivers would include Jim Clark, Peter Arundell and Trevor Taylor. Clearly, the 2-litre GT class was going to be very competitive!"

While the Ian Walker Racing équipe had the cream of Team Lotus talent on speed-dial, Warner was also able to call upon a works driver in the shape of former tank commander Mike Spence. In the sister 26R would be a talented Scot who had claimed 14 wins the previous year in a variety of hardware, scoring at least one victory at every circuit he visited. Jackie Young Stewart, who at that point was better known for being the brother of former racer Ian Stewart, was still some way short of becoming a Grand Prix colossus. However, the '64 season would help cement the 25-year-old's reputation as a driver with a gilded future ahead of him.

Future Formula One superstar Jackie Stewart joined the 'Flag for the 1964 season. He would dovetail sportscar outings with an F3 campaign with Ken Tyrrell.

A Chequered Life

Warner battled fatigue and hallucinations as he drove night and day on the 1964 Monte Carlo Rally.

For the boss, 1964 would prove a bittersweet season; one which kicked off in unfamiliar fashion as he participated in his first-ever rally. It would also be his last. With the Chequered Flag acting as London Reliant agents, Warner's inclusion in the factory team's attack on January's Monte Carlo Rally seemed logical, even if his achievements trackside were no guarantee of him performing well off-piste. It would prove a tough baptism. "Reliant was running a three-car team that year with the Sabre 6 model. Each car had a modified Ford Zephyr straight-six engine with a Raymond Mays alloy cylinder head, three twin-choke Weber carbs, a Servais exhaust and loads of other bits; there was plenty of poke, that's for sure, but the handling was poor.

"On top of that, the organisers penalised GT cars by adding a hefty five per cent to the special stage times under the supposed equivalency formula. I drove from Chiswick to the Reliant factory in Tamworth, then in the rally car up to Glasgow via the Lake District to join the other team cars for the midnight start. We arrived at Dover in the early hours and landed in France to be greeted with freezing fog but, by focusing the four 'flamethrower' spotlights on the verge a few feet ahead, I could just about keep going. I soon had the other Glasgow starters in convoy behind me, which caused chaos when I took a right fork which turned out to be a farm track. Everyone then had to back up onto the road. If nothing else, this did rouse the co-driver, who to that point had slept for most of the way. My 'navigator,' Peter Roberts, never once took the wheel, so I had to drive all the road transit sections in addition to the competition stages. That was all the way to Monte Carlo, his instructions consisting primarily of 'follow those cars.'

"In those days, rallies really were gruelling. I drove non-stop day and night apart from the few service stops. Even then, it was impossible to so much as catnap, as fascinated locals insisted on continuously knocking on the Sabre's glassfibre body to see how strong it was. There was one special stage which ran down an access road towards a quarry; it was covered in mist and I was completely exhausted and dehydrated. I can clearly recall seeing a uniformed gendarme with white gauntlets beckoning me to stop at a halt sign. I did as instructed, which once again roused my co-driver – who couldn't see the fuzz: it was an illusion. I was hallucinating! It was all very dangerous. In fact my Reliant team-mates Bobby Parkes and Arthur Senior went off the road descending the Col de Turini the very next day. They tumbled 70ft end-over-end down a mountainside, before coming to a halt. The Sabre's glassfibre body looked like Shredded Wheat, with only the railway carriage-like chassis and the race harnesses stopping them from suffering more than black eyes and bloody noses. Roberts and I eventually came home in 94th place, which was enough for fourth in class. I was then

Right: Reliant team-mates Bobby Parkes and Arthur Senior were fortunate to walk away from a 70ft tumble on the Col du Turini stage.

Graham Warner completed the distance in the 1964 Monte Carlo Rally, but had no desire to drive his Sabre 6 back to Reliant's factory in Tamworth. He's seen here with 'nominal' co-driver Peter Roberts.

asked by someone at Reliant if I would mind driving the car back from Monaco to Tamworth. By now I'd had my fill of rallying and declined. I flew home."

Intriguingly, fifth in class in a privateer Sabre 6 was another Graham Warner, whose wife was also called Shirley …

Graham Arthur Warner returned to more familiar surroundings on March 30 for the traditional Easter Monday BARC International meeting at Goodwood. A single 26R was fielded for Mike Spence for the 15-lap Sussex Trophy race for GT cars. While Graham Hill emerged victorious aboard the Maranello Concessionaires Ferrari 250GTO, the 1600cc class witnessed a tremendous Lotus battle between Peter Arundell and Spence. A mere 0.4sec separated the 26R duo, with the former just edging out his rival. Warner himself stepped up for the national meeting at Oulton Park on April 11. "The arrangement I had was that I would drive whenever Mike or Jackie were unavailable. At Oulton I started back in 22nd place after a halfshaft U/J failed in practice, but managed to battle through to finish second to Jim Clark in the IWR car. I then drove the car at the following month's *Daily Express* International Trophy meeting."

While Jack Brabham claimed honours in the headline non-championship Grand Prix, the May 2 programme kicked off with a wet GT race. With IWR and the 'Flag both fielding two cars apiece, the battle for the 1150cc-1600cc class was settled early on as Clark blasted into an unassailable lead, with Arundell making it an IWR one-two. Stewart finished third in class following a first lap spin. For the 'Flag principal, it was a case of what might have been. "I led all the other Elans into Stowe Corner for the first time and then a wheel fell off. Nobody had noticed that the Lotus kit had been supplied with two left-hand front hubs. The mechanics just tightened them up in the direction of the little arrows on the spinners!"

Stewart was back in a 26R for the Mallory Park meeting on May 17. Dovetailing his Lotus outings with a Formula Three campaign with Ken Tyrrell's Cooper squad, the rising star claimed single-seater honours before wrapping up the up-to-1600cc GT prize for the 'Flag. He led from the get-go, but for the entire ten-lap distance he had the IWR 'Gold Bug' 26R of Arundell in his mirrors. Stewart countered his every move to pull clear of the similar Chris Barber-owned car driven by Mike Beckwith and the second 'Flag entry of Spence, with the top four places remaining constant to the end. *Autosport*'s Gregor Grant reported: "Stewart drove with exquisite precision, and a man who can beat Peter Arundell in a similar car must really have something! So hard did Arundell press the Scotsman that Jackie turned in a new 1600cc lap record of 55.2sec, 88.04mph."

Stewart was also on scintillating form at the Jaguar Drivers' Club meeting at Crystal Palace on April 15. Displaying his customary versatility, he kicked off his Saturday with victory in the 35-lap Pontin Trophy race aboard John Coombs' 'Lightweight' Jaguar E-type. He then stepped into the much smaller Lotus to repeat the feat in the 15-lap 1600cc GT car race. Starting from pole, he had no IWR opposition to contend with this time around. Nonetheless, the run up to the race had been filled with drama after a rubber suspension doughnut broke in practice. Warner had been due to drive the sister car, but instead it was cannibalised to make Stewart's Lotus drivable. The Scot then completed his personal hat-trick by winning the Jaguar Saloons and XKs race aboard Eric Brown's hot XK120.

The team's subsequent outing would be the Ilford Trophy GT race at Brands Hatch on July 11. It's a race which is etched on Warner's memory. "It's one that has passed into motorsport folklore. The pole-sitting Cobra failed to make the grid so others – Roy Salvadori in Tommy Atkins' similar car, Jackie in the Coombs E-type, and Jack Sears in the Willment Cobra – all moved up a place on the grid. But this moved Sears from the second row to the first. In the race he was black-flagged after two laps for taking the wrong grid slot and pitted, to then be sent on his way – he was by now quite furious – to carve his way through the field. His entrant John Willment – a hot-tempered man for whom I had little time – then had a heated altercation with RAC steward Dean Delamont. Willment proceeded to push Delamont into a flower box and consequently lost his entrant's licence. Jack then drove like a man possessed and came up on my Lotus and the Porsche 904 of Dickie Stoop, passing us in one sideways move after Hawthorn Bend before passing in turn Jackie Oliver and John Whitmore who had been drafted into the IWR team for the race. They had been tucked up behind Peter Proctor who was driving our other car in place of Jackie. To the delight of the crowd, Sears carried on overtaking everyone and beat Jackie to the win. Proctor, who drove very well indeed, finished fifth overall, broke the class lap record and won the 2-litre class from Whitmore, Oliver, Stoop and myself."

The boss' next outing would be the 37-lap GT race at the Archie Scott Brown meeting at Snetterton on July 20. Driving the lone 'Flag entry in the oversubscribed headliner, Warner battled Oliver's 26R for 1151-1600cc class honours and was ahead at three-quarter distance, only to abruptly retire on the 28th tour when the differential seized solid. With Stewart and Spence spearheading the team's attack on the 2.5-litre Redex Trophy race at the Guards International Trophy meeting at Brands Hatch on Monday August 3, nobody could get near the former's practice time of 1min 50.6sec. Following 53 racing miles, he came home comfortably ahead of Spence, who was equally untroubled in second place, despite his car emitting plumes of smoke.

Warner wouldn't be quite as lucky at the end of the month as he returned to Zandvoort for the latest round of the European Cup Challenge series. Expected to feature in the 30-lap GT car finale, Warner spun LOV1 on the opening tour. Admitting to *Autosport* that "It was handling rather peculiarly," he came home an eventual second in class behind the similar car of Belgian Jean Wauters. Though not the result he was hoping for, this international foray at least partially made up for his disappointment at not competing in the Nürburgring 1000km in May of that year. After being offered a drive alongside Mike Beckwith in the Lotus belonging to jazz legend Chris Barber, the car was scratched from the race after its engine blew in practice.

The visit to The Netherlands would be Warner's final overseas foray as a driver; it marked his final race start of any description. "Because I only drove the 26Rs when either Jackie or Mike was unavailable, the big problem for me was that the cars were each set up differently. They were prepared to suit the driver's preferences and neither setup suited my style of driving. And with the pressure of running a business as well as a race team, I decided to hang up my crash hat."

The 'Flag rounded out the year in the best way possible, with Spence claiming a convincing win in the 2-litre GT race at the Goodwood Tourist Trophy meeting on August 29. The Croydon-born up-and-comer led home Porsche man Dickie Stoop by 13.2sec following 21 largely untroubled laps. It marked the end of the team's Elan programme with '64 honours being largely even between Ian Walker Racing and the 'The Tattered Rag,' as it was christened by its rival. Warner recalls: "The Walker cars had a stiffening subframe of half-inch square tubing welded inside the backbone chassis but I thought that would contravene regulations. The 26R's balance remained better if the circuit was damp or wet as the cornering forces generated were lower than on a dry circuit, so the chassis flexing was not so pronounced. Our cars

Warner was back in a 'Flag Lotus for the Archie Scott Brown meeting at Snetterton in July 1964. He got ahead of Jackie Oliver's similar car in the GT race, only to retire his car after the diff seized.

Nobody could touch Jackie Stewart in the 2.5-litre Redex Trophy race at the August 1964 Guards International Trophy meeting at Brands Hatch. He led home team-mate Mike Spence.

were subsequently sold to Mark Konig, who was the sales manager at Maranello Concessionaires [and future founder of the Nomad marque], and his sister/racer Gabriel.

"Overall it wasn't a bad season and Mike and Jackie drove well. Of course both went on to have Formula One careers, with Mike's being tragically cut short by a practice crash in the run-up the '68 Indy 500. Jackie was obviously a star in the making. You only had to look at his results in Formula Three to know he was destined for the big time. The following year he was a Grand Prix driver with BRM, and the rest is history. And while I cannot claim to have landed

And overleaf: Warner's last ever competitive start was at the August 1964 Zandvoort for a round of the European Cup Challenge. After spinning his Lotus on the first lap, he tore through the field to finish second in class.

him the drive with British Racing Motors, I can say that I put in a good word for him. At the end of '64 I was summoned to the Dorchester Hotel for tea with 'Lord' Louis Stanley and his wife Jean. She was the sister of Sir Alfred Owen who was chairman of the Owen Group which owned the BRM team. I was grilled about Jackie; was he 'one of us,' or 'the right sort?' I answered in the affirmative on both counts. I'm fairly sure they already had their minds made up about him and just wanted a little insider info. Short of him eating his peas from the wrong side of the fork he was always going to get the drive."

The 1965 season would mark a return to single-seaters, the team dovetailing a Formula Three campaign with selected sports car outings with an AC Cobra. Up-and-coming Briton Roger Mac, and Roy Pike, would be armed with Brabham BT16s, the latter having already made a big impression in junior formulae since his arrival in the UK in 1961. It also marked a return, of sorts, Pike having previously won for the Gemini marque.

The '65 season began at Oulton Park on April 3 and the Mid-Cheshire Motor Club's *Daily Express*-sponsored Spring International meeting. While works Brabham man Denny Hulme won the banner Formula Two event at record speed, Pike was also on blistering form. *Autosport*'s Gregor Grant wrote: 'In his Brabham-Ford, [he] literally ran away with the 19-lap Formula 3 race – the fastest ever run at Oulton Park – and set up new figures of 1min 46.2sec (93.59mph) to beat Jackie Stewart's 1964 record by 1.4sec." He finished 12.4sec ahead of second-place man Charlie Crichton-Stuart, with Mac's outings in the category becoming intermittent as the season progressed, and he looked instead to Formula Two.

Continuing from where he left off, Pike was on victorious form in the lone 'Flag Brabham at the April 19 Easter Goodwood meeting despite hail, sleet and snow doing its best to disrupt proceedings. On race day, the Chichester Cup thrash was halted early on as weather took a turn for the Biblical, with Pike and Piers Courage battling it out at the restart. Pike's margin of victory on this occasion would be 0.6sec. Mac, meanwhile, claimed honours in the Sussex Trophy event for GT cars with Peter Sutcliffe's ex-David Piper Ferrari 250GTO at close quarters for 36 racing miles. Later that month Pike, running the Brabham under the California Racing Partnership banner, took his third win from as many starts with Formula Three honours at the Pau Grand Prix meeting. Starting from pole, he headed home Mauro Bianchi's Alpine, also taking the fastest lap for good measure.

Mac was back in the Cobra for the RAC Tourist Trophy race on April 1, this the thirtieth running of the prestigious event, venturing north for the first time as 37,000 spectators flocked to Oulton Park for the two 2-hour sports car races. While Denny Hulme would emerge as overall winner aboard Sid Taylor's Brabham BT8, the battle in the GT class was far from clear cut. In the opening instalment, battle raged between Mac's AC and the John Danway Racing Ferrari 250GTO of Mike Salmon, the former pitting on the thirteenth tour for fuel. The young charger then set about returning to the front, only to have a wheel come away on the approach to Island Bend. The following day Pike made it four wins on the trot with overall honours in the Grand Prix de Magny-Cours F3 race over Mike Knight's Cooper. A week later, he would suffer a rare defeat at Zolder, taking the first heat but finishing second overall on aggregate to the Charles Lucas Engineering Brabham BT10 of Jonathan Williams.

Pike's packed programme continued at Silverstone on May 15 for the prestigious BRDC International Trophy meeting. Piers Courage took the lead at the start of the Formula Three support race and stayed at the front over the 25-lap distance, with the main point of focus for spectators being the early battle for second between Pike, Williams and Merlyn driver John Fenning. Williams' car retired on lap 18 with a broken fuel pump, with Fenning slowing in the closing stages, allowing Pike an uninterrupted dash to the runner-up spot.

Then came a return visit to Monaco for the May 29 Grand Prix support race. This round-the-houses classic had, during its Formula Junior incarnation, proved a source of misery for the 'Flag, and the '65 running for Formula Three cars were no different. John Cardwell won the opening heat in his Goodwin Racing Brabham, the second heat marking the appearance of hard-charging American sports car star Bob Bondurant in the principality. He dominated his practice session aboard Ken Tyrrell's Cooper T76, with Pike lining up alongside him to make it an all-US front row. An American driver would emerge the victor, but it would be Peter Revson. Pike held the lead for 15 laps of the 16-lap heat, only to clash with Bondurant outside the Hotel de Paris. Revson then claimed the final aboard Ron Harris' Lotus.

While Pike rued missing out on Monaco glory, he was on form for the Whit meeting at Brands Hatch on June 6, where £500 was on offer to the winner of the 20-lap Formula Three race. Predictably, this extra

Roy Pike slides his 'Flag Brabham out of the chicane at Goodwood during the 1965 Easter meeting ahead of Piers Courage's similar car. The American would lead to the flag to take the Chichester Cup.

A Chequered Life

Roger Mac tamed the Chequered Flag's ex-Tommy Atkins Cobra to win the Sussex Trophy race at Goodwood over the 1965 Easter weekend.

incentive triggered some intense lappery from the frontrunners, with the first 11 cars on the grid bettering the existing lap record on the venue's short circuit. Courage, Pike and Crichton-Stuart blanketed the front row and they would finish in that order, but the bare facts belie the frenzied battle that raged between the latter duo. Courage got the drop on his rivals at the start, with Crichton-Stuart holding down second place until three-quarter distance. As Nick Brittan reported in *Autosport*: "Crichton-Stuart and Pike [then] came up to lap a couple of backmarkers. Pike swooped and, screwing his courage into a small ball, did the lot in one fell swoop at Bottom Bend. It took Chichton-Stuart half a lap to clear the two tail-enders but by then the crafty Californian was away and gone."

Pike then went one better in the Redex Trophy race for large-displacement GT cars. This race marked his maiden outing in the 'Flag Cobra, not that he was overawed by the differences between a 1-litre single-seater and a 4.7-litre V8 sports car: "People say Cobras were hairy. Everyone makes a big deal about these things but it wasn't particularly scary. I had raced Austin-Healeys beforehand, and the Cobra was much the same – a wallowy muscle car. You just adapted to suit. I had some prior experience of driving a Cobra. A year earlier I had tested the Willment Cobra coupé at Goodwood. Tony Maggs drove it too. They then got Ken Miles over. He was the big Cobra racer and development man. I was sent to the airport to meet him. He was an ex-pat Brit trying to be American and I was talking out the side of my mouth trying to be British. It was back to Goodwood again where Miles hit the chicane before saying it wasn't fast enough and going home. Graham's Cobra, by comparison, was a bit more like a road car. I enjoyed driving the Cobra as you had to work quite hard to get the best out of it but I always preferred single-seaters which were so precise and responsive by comparison."

Following an epic battle with John Miles' Diva, Pike tamed the Cobra for a debut win. A day later, Mac drove the car to third place and a class win in the BARC's sports car thrash at Goodwood. However, luck deserted him on his return to Formula Three: he retired from the ten-lap Reg Parnell Trophy race on the penultimate tour with engine problems, while early leader Pike came home an uncharacteristically low eighth overall following a spin.

The 25-year-old American returned to his winning ways for the British Grand Prix meeting on July 10. As Richard Feast noted in *Autosport*: "Roy Pike drove with the stamp of a master to win the Formula Three race for the BRDC Trophy … the Chequered Flag driver led from lap one to lap 20, this time lowering the lap record by 0.2-seconds." Two weeks later, he was back in Northamptonshire for the Aston Martin Owners' Club meeting, only to retire his car from the oversubscribed Club Trophy race with a broken fuel pump just three laps in. The same issue hobbled the sister Brabham of new incumbent Chris Irwin. While Chris Amon ran out the winner in the headline Martini International Trophy sports car race in his McLaren M1A, Pike's Cobra spent much of the 40 laps trying to fend off Keith St John's Elva Mk7S, which ultimately retired with a blown head gasket. Once clear, Pike ran out the remaining laps to place sixth overall and second in class to David Piper's Ferrari 250LM. However, a degree of confusion surrounded the final scores, some reports suggested that Pike had been the victim of a timekeeping error, and had actually finished fourth.

Pike's luck would desert him completely at the 'Flag's next outing – the BARC Bromley Bowl meeting at Crystal Palace on July 31. He retired the Cobra from the GT race with an expensive-looking hole in the block. Just to pile on the misery, he was forced out of the opening Formula Three heat after the Brabham's suspension collapsed in the middle of North Tower bend. Irwin emerged as the unchallenged winner, and then enjoyed a tussle with Peter Gethin's Charles Lucas Engineering BT10 in the opening stages of the final before claiming honours after his rival's engine let go. This victory would prove the first of many for Irwin and the 'Flag.

The Londoner would consolidate his standing the following month during his first overseas foray for the team at Karlskoga, Sweden. The August 8 meeting, which also hosted a round of the European Touring Car Championship, saw the Wandsworth man keep his head while all those around him were busy losing theirs. He led from start to finish as chaos ensued behind him.

With a new small-block Ford V8 installed in the Cobra, a new – and unexpected – pilot was installed for the Guards International Trophy meeting at Brands Hatch on Monday, August 30. Roy Pike's Monaco nemesis Bob Bondurant was on hand for the Redex Trophy GT support race. "He had a reputation in the US as being *the* Cobra man," Warner recalls. "We thought we would give him a try and maybe we could learn from his experiences racing for the factory Shelby Cobra team. He was a decent enough driver but rather hard on the equipment."

The Californian comfortably placed the car on pole, scorching away from the noon start to head Jack Sears' Willment Cobra with Peter Lumsden's proven 'Lightweight' E-type in third. The two Cobras gradually eased their way clear of the Jaguar, with Bondurant seemingly in command. However, shortly before half-distance the lead Cobra began to slow as the clutch began to slip. The problem persisted, with Sears and his pursuers all leapfrogging the ailing black and white Cobra, which retired before the end. Pike, meanwhile, had managed only two laps as he guested in Julian Sutton's Lotus Elan, a puncture ending play at Bottom Bend.

However, Pike was back on track for the British Empire Trophy race, which saw a combined field of Formula Two and Formula Three cars vie for honours. Jim Clark emerged as the overall winner in his Ron Harris/Team Lotus 35-Cosworth, with Pike establishing a category record to place thirteenth on the road and first in class. One place behind him was Irwin, who was back in a Merlyn Mk9 after his 'Flag Brabham developed a problem with its engine.

The same ailment struck both 'Flag cars intermittently at Zandvoort during the August 29 *Autosport* & Dunlop Trophy race, with Irwin finishing third behind Kurt Ahrens and Trevor Blokdyk, with a down-on-power Pike fifth behind Australian privateer Martin Davies in what became a Brabham benefit. Two weeks later, Irwin was back on crushing form, claiming two of three heats in the Coupe de l'Avenir race at Zolder, Belgium, while placing second in the third behind local Cooper driver Jacques Bernusset. He comfortably won outright on aggregate, with an embattled Pike down in tenth.

The roles would be reversed back on the British mainland as the team-mates descended on Oulton Park for the International Gold Cup meeting. While John Surtees bested Denny Hulme by the narrowest of margins to win the headline Gold Cup encounter for the Midland Racing Partnership, the Formula Three thrash that preceded it provided almost as big a spectacle. Irwin appeared to have the race sewn up until tail-enders came into play. With Pike in second place, working hard to fend off a determined John Fenning, Irwin was comfortably in charge until he

A Chequered Life

Cobra star Bob Bondurant was brought in to drive the team's Cobra for the August 1965 Guards International Trophy meeting. He made an immediate impression.

came up on a backmarker shortly after half-distance. He exited Old Hall with deranged front suspension, his race over. Pike was then left to bat away Fenning's Cooper, *Autosport* reporting that "… a calculated risk with bottom gear at a second-gear corner got him well clear with a few laps to go, and he won by just over five seconds with a new lap record under his belt."

Pike was on pole for the 'Flag's penultimate meeting of the '65 season at Brands Hatch on October 1. Piers Courage got the drop on him at the start of the 20-lap Motor Racing Silver Salver Trophy dash, only to retire his car with a broken gearbox before quarter-distance. Irwin, who had made up several places after a tardy start, then assumed the lead with Pike following. Irwin was untroubled to the end, with Pike retiring his Brabham on the fourteenth tour with an oil leak.

The '65 season ended with a three-car tilt at the BRSCC Boxing Day meeting at Brands Hatch with Irwin now armed with the latest Brabham BT16 running on Goodyear rubber. Pike continued with the Dunlop-shod BT16 with Mac back in action following his Reims shunt in the sister car. But it would be a Piers Courage benefit in the 15-lap Lombank Trophy race, with Irwin finishing second five seconds down with Pike fourth behind Team Lotus man Ray Parsons. Mac's comeback drive ended with a broken driveshaft just three laps in.

Warner recalls: "While it wasn't a victorious end to the year, 1965 had been the Chequered Flag's most successful season to date. The team had won more than fifty per cent of the races it started. We were very confident going into 1966."

The tiny promotional Elan model was intended for sponsors and drivers. Just six were made.

VIII. On a winning streak

Bolstered by its strongest season yet, the Chequered Flag earned official works status for 1966 after it was picked to run factory Brabhams in Formula Three. Warner explains: "My plan had been to continue with Roy Pike and Chris Irwin, but Roy was poached by Colin Chapman: Charles Lucas would run the Formula 3 team on behalf of Team Lotus, and Roy would drive alongside Piers Courage. We kept hold of Chris, though, who at that time was unquestionably the brightest British prospect in the category. We had run Roger Mac again at the end of '65, and also looked after his F2 Brabham. He stepped back down to do Formula Three with us in order to try and rebuild his career following his shunt at Reims the previous year."

Keen to maintain a presence in the GT category, Warner also retained the existing 4.7-litre AC Cobra, and reached an agreement with veteran competitor Paul Pycroft to purchase a 7-litre version. "The deal was that we would acquire the car together. We bought it off *Autosport*'s Paddy McNally: the 'Flag would prepare it and Paul would use it for hillclimbing, which left us clear to race the car in international Group 4 GT races. It was a proper Cobra 427 from Shelby American. It was a terrible car to begin with, though. It boiled its *oil* during the first test at Silverstone. Over the course of the season we went through the whole thing, adding a much larger, fully-ducted oil cooler. We also ducted a larger alloy radiator which cured the chronic overheating, and also did a lot to improve the suspension and brakes."

There was, however, one slight problem with running such a broad spectrum of cars – the existing transporter could only hold two at a time, so Warner dug deep and ordered a new, much larger truck. "We bought a Ford D400 chassis, to which was added a body of our own design." It would get plenty of use, zigzagging the Continent during the course of the season.

The team's race card didn't get off to a flier as the snowy April 2 BARC 200 meeting at Oulton Park was abandoned; Irwin had been second to Peter Gethin in practice. Two days later, Mac was testing at Goodwood only to get caught up in another monstrous shunt after Mike De Udy's Porsche spun in front of him. Mac had nowhere to go, his Brabham BT18 leaving the road in avoidance before turning over. "Fortunately Roger wasn't injured, just badly bruised and somewhat shaken," Warner recalls. "The car was a mess, though. The next meeting was the following weekend which meant more all-nighters for the mechanics and they effectively built a new car in only a few days."

The hard work paid off. The season proper kicked off at Goodwood on April 11, Irwin emerging victorious

The team replaced its ageing transporter with this new custom-bodied Ford D400 for the 1966 season.

Roger Mac stepped down to F3 for 1966, but had departed the 'Flag team before the end of the season.

in the Chichester Cup race for Formula Three cars ahead of John Fenning and Gethin. Mac finished sixth, just behind Pike and pole-sitter Brian Hart, following a race-long conflict for fourth place. Unfortunately, the season was about to take another turn. A day after the Goodwood victory, chief mechanic Bill Granger, along with youthful spanner-man John Jackson, loaded the Brabhams into the old bus-based transporter and departed for Italy. Irwin and Mac were entered in the April 24 Gran Premio Fina two-parter, which supported the 1000km sports car race at Monza, and the Vigorelli Trophy at the same venue on May 1. However, the journey to Italy would prove somewhat testing for chief mechanic Granger.

"The plan was to drive down through Germany, Switzerland and up to Andermatt before heading over the Gotthard pass," he recalls. "Unfortunately, it snowed heavily on the way up and the pass was closed. We stopped at a hotel and the transporter was spinning its wheels just getting into the car park. The hotel owner then mentioned that there was a train station at the bottom of the hill; if we could get down there, we could then catch a train which ran all the way into Italy.

"I then phoned Graham who, to be fair, couldn't really do anything. He wished us luck, and told me to call him if we made it to Monza. 'Young John' was a lovely guy and very enthusiastic, but it really was just us. We then had the small matter of turning the transporter around. Fortunately for us, the hotel was full of kids on a school trip. We got them to push on the back and the sides, and we managed, somehow, to spin it around. Then there was the small matter of all those hairpins on our descent. What a drive that was! We eventually managed to get a train from Göschenen to Oriolo before heading for Monza, only for a wheel bearing to go en route to the hotel – ker-klunk, ker-klunk ... The following morning, it took about three hours to drive no distance at all to the circuit. When we got there, I decided to reverse in and pull up to the fence so that we could get the cars out and I could work on the wheel bearing. The officials opened the gate – we were the first team

Bob Bondurant was on hand for the May 1966 Ilford 500 race at Brands Hatch, sharing the team's 7-litre Cobra with sports car veteran David Piper.

A Chequered Life

The ever-versatile Roy Pike returned to the team to race the small-block Cobra for the 500-mile sports car race at Brands Hatch.

to arrive – and then the wheel came off and tucked itself under the hub, so we were now blocking the entrance. Some repair guys from Monza turned up in a truck, but began pontificating about insurance. After two hours' worth of aggravation, we'd had enough, so I took a large jack from the truck and got on with it amid much gesticulation from the Italians. John then got behind the wheel while I effectively steered the thing – on cobbles – using the jack. I've had better days ..."

With the team failing to make many friends in the run-up to the event, Irwin further upset the locals by winning his heat, with Mac coming fourth. However, Mac came unstuck in the final during a furious slipstreaming battle. As the lead pack descended upon backmarkers for the first time, a spooked tailender darted into his path. The unsighted Mac struck the back of the car, launching his Brabham end-over-end. He was thrown clear of his car, and was fortunate to sustain only cracked ribs and asphalt burns. Irwin also got caught up in the melee, dropping to an eventual fifth on aggregate with Mac still placing seventh despite his crash. Cosmopolitan British ace Jonathan Williams maintained some Italian honour, winning outright for Roman marque De Sanctis.

With Mac out of action, Irwin became the sole 'Flag representative for the repeat visit to Monza. He would win his heat and place third overall behind Williams and Lola pilot Mike Beckwith, the latter having also won the previous weekend's Juan Jover Trophy in Barcelona. Irwin would be without a team-mate for the Les Leston Trophy race at Brands Hatch on May 8, where he finished fifth before hopping into the small-block Cobra for the headline 500 mile sports car enduro. Sharing the driving for one race only would be 'Flag old boy Roy Pike. Bob Bondurant was also back on side, joined by David Piper in the big-block Cobra 427. "David had shown himself to be a good, reliable driver in long-distance events, which is what we needed for this one," Warner recalls.

The race was run in appalling conditions, with Innes Ireland among the big names to venture into the scenery at Stirling's Bend. With 80 laps run, Jackie Oliver pitted his Jaguar with a commanding lead, with Piper holding third ahead of Irwin. Oliver's good work was undone by team-mate Ken Baker, who gyrated the E-type just three laps into his stint, going off at Paddock before clouting a bank. Piper then assumed the lead, somehow keeping the twitchy 7-litre Cobra shiny side-up on the water-logged circuit. Unfortunately, hopes of a 'Flag one-two finish ended minutes later as Irwin hurriedly shot into the pits, complaining of a dramatic loss of oil – it was leaking through a large hole in the engine block. But nobody could catch the lead Cobra, Bondurant snaking the car across the line after 175 laps to beat the Peter Sutcliffe/Eric Liddell Ford GT40 – and this despite him sauntering into the pits on lap 174 in the belief that the race had already ended.

For the team principal, the victory brought with it a mixture of elation and frustration. "Before we acquired the second Cobra, we spoke to several race organisers and promoters to make sure there would be sufficient Group 4 races that year. We were assured that there would be at least ten, maybe a dozen, but throughout the season the Group 4 class was usually merged with those for Group 6 and 7

Bondurant snakes off the line for the Ilford 500 parade lap in the 7-litre Cobra, the team's sister small-block car also starting from the front row.

cars – so out-and-out racing cars rather than GTs. Either that or the class was left out altogether. The win at Brands was great, but opportunities to race competitively became increasingly rare."

The Formula Three campaign, meanwhile, continued apace with Irwin finishing only a tenth of a second behind Roy Pike after a thrilling 25-lap battle at the May 14 BRDC International Trophy meeting at Silverstone. Bondurant was fifth in the sister car. However, there were further distractions. The Dutch car manufacturer DAF had been keen to promote its Variomatic 'rubber band' transmission in motorsport, having first dipped its toe in the competitive waters with selected Formula Three outings in 1965. Warner

An elated Graham Warner flanked by Bondurant (left) and Piper (right), after winning the 1966 Ilford 500 race. It was the only international win ever achieved by a 7-litre Cobra.

recalls: "DAF, or rather the firm's chief development engineer Wim Hendriks, approached us to see if we would be interested in helping develop the transmission. They had tried installing it in an Alexis, but it didn't work too well. Hendricks knew that we'd had success with our Brabhams, and was aware that we had previously built cars ourselves, so we seemed like a good fit. I then went over to Eindhoven at the invitation of Mr Van Doorne, who was the boss at DAF.

"The deal was that the 'Flag would provide the drivers, enter the cars, prepare the chassis and so on, while DAF would look after the engines and transmissions. We did a lot of development over the course of the season and the Brabham-DAFs became reasonably competitive. The problem for us was that the Variomatic transmission was quite a bit heavier than the manual 'boxes and had a higher polar moment of inertia around the centre of gravity. There were problems when oil and road dirt got between the titanium-faced drums and the pulleys, but we helped DAF rectify that as much as possible."

The next engagement on the 'Flag's calendar was the Monaco Formula Three race on May 21 in support of the principality's Grand Prix. The team would take a Brabham quartet, two conventional gearbox cars, and also a brace of Variomatic versions for Bondurant to choose from. Irwin would lead the team, the sister BT18 being driven by Oscar 'Cacho' Fangio. "He was the son of the great Juan Manuel Fangio, the five-time Formula One World Champion," Warner recalls. "I had the great pleasure of meeting Fangio Sr and he was charming and very humble. Unfortunately, Cacho wasn't anything like as good as his father: in the race he over-revved the engine – by about 2000rpm – and retired. We never ran him again."

Irwin, meanwhile, won his heat, with Bondurant a commendable fifth. In the final, Piers Courage got the drop on Irwin, only to smite the wall at Tabac, which

Chris Irwin couldn't keep Piers Courage behind him at Brands Hatch in May 1966, finishing second to the future Grand Prix driver in the team's Brabham.

damaged his car's front suspension. Irwin locked up in avoidance, which allowed the Matra MS5 of first heat winner Jean-Pierre Beltoise to nip through. He would lead to the end, with Irwin half a second behind following 24 hotly-contested laps. Irwin's drive was all the more remarkable as his car's clutch had packed up early in the race. Sadly for Bondurant, his efforts were for nought. He was forced to retire at Casino seventeen laps in after a rival poked his car's nose into the Variomatic transmission's pulleys – for the second time – which hindered further progress.

It was back to Brands Hatch on May 29, Irwin finishing a close second to Piers Courage in the Les Leston Cup race. The plan had been to enter the Cobras for the GT race at the same meeting but, in the words of *Autosport*: "They were being bloody minded."

Both entries were scratched. A day later, the team decamped to Crystal Palace for the London Trophy meeting. Irwin took the lead at the start of the Bromley Bowl Formula Three race and held on for the entire distance. A recuperated Mac came home seventh, also competing in the headline Formula Two race, where he came home eleventh aboard his Brabham BT16. It was his second Formula Two start of the season, following a lowly tenth place finish earlier in the year in the *Sunday Mirror* Trophy race at Goodwood. His drive with the Formula Three squad had been kept open ever since his Monza shunt, with no full-time replacement being sought or found. However, Mac decided to concentrate on Formula Two, which opened the door for Mike Beckwith to take over his seat. "He was always pushing for a drive," Warner recalls. "Mike tried hard, and was available to do loads of testing with the DAF transmission. This was mainly at Zolder and Zandvoort, and DAF paid him handsomely for it."

Beckwith made an immediate impression, finishing third overall in his heat at the all-important Monza Lottery meeting, with Irwin emerging victorious. Beckwith then finished second in the final behind Jonathan Williams while Irwin's car dropped out with a blown rocker cover gasket – it was his sole retirement that year. From Monza, the team made for Rheims, John Fenning winning the frenetic Coupe de Vitesse race aboard his Tyrrell Racing Matra, with Irwin fifth and Beckwith seventh. Gregor Grant wrote in *Autosport*: "Words can scarcely describe the fantastic race for Formula Three cars, and anyone who could keep an accurate lap chart must be a genius when more than a dozen cars kept chopping and changing on every lap."

It was back to an altogether wetter Northamptonshire for the team's next outing – the AMOC Martini International Trophy meeting at Silverstone on July 9.

Mike Beckwith was recruited to drive the Brabham-DAF with its Variomatic transmission.

Future saloon car star Alec Poole made a rare single-seater appearance for the 'Flag at Silverstone in August 1966, but admitted to being too tall to be fully comfortable in the Brabham.

Unfortunately, plans to run Irwin in the feature sports car race ended a few days beforehand when Mac returned to the team to shake down the Cobra 427 at the Towcester venue. He had a major moment at Maggots, the car's V8 being reduced to shrapnel after he over-revved it. In a quote attributed to the team boss in *Autosport*, this "… was the end of a lot of things."

It proved one Mac-related incident too many for an exasperated Warner. Nonetheless, the same meeting did see the 'Flag's first 1-2 finish of the season as Beckwith narrowly pipped an aggrieved Irwin – who was obliged to follow team orders – to win the Formula Three encounter ahead of Ken Tyrrell's latest find, Jacky Ickx, who had started at the back of the field.

Beckwith then became the sole 'Flag ambassador at the fifth Critérium de Vitesse de Magny Cours Formula Three race on July 17. His Brabham-DAF, now in black and white with an orange nose to denote its Dutch connections, finished third in the damp opening heat, Paul Watson gushed in *Autosport*: "The DAF transmission was causing a clash between engine braking and actual braking, and poor Mike was having to sort all this out even before he set the car up properly for the corner. In other words, he was in fact taking two corners instead of one on every occasion, but still putting in some of the most polished driving."

Despite his sterling efforts, Beckwith had no answer for the Alpines of outright winner Robby Weber and Mauro Bianchi, or the Matra MS5 of third place man Johnny Servoz-Gavin, instead having to be content with the honour of being the first non-Frenchman home in the final. The following weekend, it was back to Silverstone and a round of the WD & HO Wills Trophy series, Beckwith finishing a lowly twelfth on aggregate. Three 'Flag Brabhams were entered for this club meeting, with future F1 driver Tim Schenken placing eighth overall. Mini ace Alec Poole was classified as seventeenth aboard the third BT18. "The drive came out of the blue," Poole recalls. "It was a great opportunity, but I was too tall for single-

A delighted Chris Irwin is flanked by Peter Sellers and Britt Ekland on the parade lap after winning the F3 race at Crystal Palace in August 1966.

seaters. I also weighed about 16 stone, so I didn't so much sit in the car as wear it."

"Schenken was working for us around that time, and we had helped out with a hot Ford Anglia he was building in our workshop," Warner recalls. "I was always being badgered by people to let them have a drive, and we ran Tim at Silverstone, but he didn't do brilliantly. He was pretty inexperienced, though. Alec was a good driver but we only ran him a few times."

The Irishman stayed with the squad for a second outing at Crystal Palace on August 6, joining Irwin and Beckwith for the 25-lap Peter Sellers Trophy race. Robin Widdows annexed pole position for the race named after the comedic actor and sometime backer of driver/engine builder Brian Hart. It was Irwin who claimed the spoils following a stellar wet weather drive to finish ahead of Peter Gethin and Roy Pike. Beckwith, who was aboard a Brabham-DAF, was running with the lead pack for much of the race, only to be jumped by the Lotus 41s of Derek Bell and Jackie Oliver after his car's engine began to lose power in the closing stages. Poole came home eleventh, just behind Hart. An elated Irwin received the trophy from Sellers but, according to some witnesses, he was altogether keener to share the lap of honour with Sellers' 24-year-old wife, Britt Ekland!

The transporter was then loaded up again for the long haul to the twisty Roskilde Ring for the August 13-14 Danish Grand Prix for Formula Three cars. The previous year's winner Irwin dominated a meeting that was blighted by some 'forceful' driving, winning all three heats before scorching to victory in the final. His team-mate Beckwith finished seventh on aggregate in his Variomatic-equipped Brabham-Ford, having had an off in his second heat following a particularly robust challenge from a local driver. A week later, Irwin scored another repeat win, dominating the 20-lap Formula Three race at Karlskoga in central Sweden from pole, with Beckwith an unfortunate retiree after his car's nose was truncated during an early skirmish.

It was then back to Kent for the Guards International Trophy meeting at Brands Hatch on August 29, Irwin finishing second behind Piers Courage with Beckwith third. Irwin also raced the big-block Cobra in the sports car encounter, but finished way down the order. Pike, meanwhile, retired the small-block Cobra from the same race. The 'Flag's hard-pressed transporter then made for Holland and the Zandvoort Trophée race on September 4 where Irwin and Jacky Ickx slugged it out for 24 laps, with the Briton heading the Belgian across the line by just 0.4sec. Ickx then joined the 'Flag for the following weekend's Coupe de l'Avenir Formula Three event at Zolder. His hopes of a win on home soil had appeared unlikely in the run-up to the meeting, as Warner recalls. "His Matra had been damaged so we offered him our spare Brabham. Obviously he went on to win the Le Mans 24 Hours six times, but even at that stage it was obvious that he had something extra. He was a very nice, cultured young man and at Zolder he gave Chris a hard time.

A DAF F3 car under construction in the Chequered Flag workshop.

Left: Warner in discussion with Chris Irwin, who he rated as a potential F1 World Champion prior to his career-ending crash aboard an Alan Mann Ford sports-prototype.

Graham Warner explains the DAF 'rubber band' transmission to Dennis Jenkinson at Pau, while Jack Brabham looks over his shoulder.

On aggregate Chris beat Jacky with Mike third in the Variomatic car. It was our first-ever 1-2-3 finish."

On September 11 both Cobras participated in the 500km Zeltweg round of the World Sports Car Championship held on the airfield circuit in Styria, Austria – if only briefly, as Jon Raeburn retired the small-block car with a split oil-cooler. "He was our used car sales manager at Chiswick for a few years, and like Schenken and many others from 'Down Under,' he kept pressing me for a drive," Warner recalls.

Bob Bondurant, meanwhile, failed to complete the opening tour in the sister car following a catastrophic loss of oil pressure. The following weekend saw Irwin finish third on aggregate in the Coupe de Vitesse three-parter at the Bugatti circuit at Le Mans behind Johnny Servoz-Gavin and Roy Pike. Beckwith was a non-finisher after a missed shift buzzed the engine.

The 'Flag's '66 season ended with the RAC European Formula Three Challenge Trophy meeting at Brands Hatch on October 2. This often chaotic event consisted of two ten-lap heats, which decided grid positions for the 35-lap final. With the cream of young international talent descending on Kent, the 'Flag pulled out all the stops by running two conventional Brabhams for Irwin and works Alfa Romeo man Andrea de Adamich, and Variomatic cars for Beckwith and Jonathan Williams. Irwin rounded out a stellar season by winning on aggregate, with Beckwith ninth – one place ahead of de Adamich. Williams was an embattled thirteenth.

It had been a remarkable campaign for the Chiswick squad, the team chief recalling: "We won nineteen races that year, seventeen of them with Chris who was an extraordinary talent. Of the many drivers who raced for us, Jim Clark and Jackie Stewart were excellent, but in 1966 I would have put money on Chris joining them as a multiple F1 World Champion. Alongside Mike Parkes, who was a superb driver and a brilliant development man, I would rate Chris as perhaps the best driver we ever ran. Sadly, he had a terrible sports car accident at the Nürburgring in 1968 and was never the same man again.

"1966 was Chris' year, but you also had to take your hat off to our mechanics Bill Granger, who left us at the end of the season, and John Jackson. We had 63 Formula Three starts, and only six retirements all year. On top of that, we had a 90 per cent reliability record across the board. That's an incredible strike rate and, when you also consider the amount of miles they put in driving to-and-fro across Europe, that percentage was all the all more remarkable. It was a great season."

Tentative plans for 1967 centred on joining forces with Charles Lucas to field Piers Courage and another in Formula Two. "'Luke' was a super chap and had done a good job running the works Lotus 41s in Formula Three," Warner recalls. "However, Colin Chapman royally screwed him at the end of '66 over prize money from Firestone. Roy Thomas – 'Tom the Weld' – who had left us to join Luke wasn't the violent sort at all, but he wanted to punch Chapman on the nose! It left a very sour taste in their mouths and this ultimately led Luke and Tom to start making cars themselves, their various Titan designs proving reasonably successful in future years."

The Formula Two plan soon evaporated, as did hopes of continuing in Formula Three. "Trade support was withdrawn at the end of '66 and we simply couldn't afford to continue. Formula Three at that time attracted numerous manufacturers, engine builders, tyre manufacturers, and of course drivers; if you didn't have the right combination you would instantly become an 'also ran.' The pace of development in the late '60s was extraordinary. The car sales business at that time was doing okay, but not to the point where I could sink a fortune into a big motorsport programme. We decided to sell the small-block Cobra and run only the 427 version in selected races in '67. DAF was keen for us to develop and run its Formula Three cars, so we put together a programme which it funded."

The 1967 season kicked off with the April 2 Coupe de Vitesse contest at the torturous Pau circuit in southwest France. A single Ford-powered Brabham-DAF BT21 was fielded for Mike Beckwith, who proved blisteringly quick in practice, his best lap being half a second faster than second-place man Jean-Pierre Jaussaud's in his works Matra. Unfortunately, the Londoner's hot laps ended abruptly with an off-road excursion that ensured he was unable to start the race – or the following weekend's Juan Jover Trophy race at Montjuïc Park in Barcelona. It was then back to Monaco for the May 6 Grand Prix support encounter. Victory in this prestigious race had eluded the 'Flag ever since its inaugural appearance back in 1961, and the '67 contest would be no different. Two latest-spec Brabham-DAF BT21s were entered for Beckwith and team returnee Roy Pike, with Formula Two hotshoe Robin Widdows being drafted in to drive the previous year's BT18. Pike and Beckwith's cars both lost oil out of the breather pipes in practice, the same issue forcing them into retirement in the final. Widdows, meanwhile, crashed out.

The May 20 AMOC Martini International Trophy

David Hobbs had a one-off outing in the team's 7-litre Cobra for the May 1967 Martini International Trophy race, and finished fourteenth.

A Chequered Life

meeting saw Pike debut the all-new Chequered Flag-built DAF in the Formula Three support race. It was the first of two cars designed and constructed by Chas Beattie and Jim Dale. "Chas designed the chassis in the time-honoured method of doing some very basic layouts on an old drawing board and then building it on the jig. I then drew it properly so that we had a record in case we bent it," Dale recalls. Pike jumped pole-sitter Harry Stiller to lead as far as Stowe corner, only to retire on the thirteenth lap after the car's undertray parted company. Beckwith, meanwhile, came home seventh. No matter, there was always sports car racing. The big-block Cobra – now wearing a distinctive hard top and the famous registration number LOV1 – was entered in the headline Group 4 contest. Grands Prix occasional David Hobbs was brought in to pilot the car. He finished fourteenth.

Beckwith was joined by another future Grand Prix victor for the June 4 Valvoline Cup at the Ring Djursland circuit in Denmark on June 4. Peter Gethin was armed with the second DAF, the long haul being for nought as he spun into retirement. Beckwith, meanwhile, finished second behind Peter Westbury in the Felday Brabham BT21. Westbury would continue where he left off with Trophée Auvergne honours at Circuit de Charade in Clermont-Ferrand two weeks later, with Beckwith being joined in France by Widdows. Armed with Brabham-DAF BT21s from earlier in the season, Beckwith claimed pole position, but crashed on the opening tour, with Widdows coming home seventh.

The team reverted back to the DAFs for the next outing, the July 2 Trophée International de la Sarthe in Le Mans. Joining Beckwith would be a man who, in future years, would triumph twice at the same venue in the 24 Hour endurance classic: Gijs van Lennep. "He was bought in because of his nationality," Warner reflects. "It helped that he was also a very useful driver. He was fast and didn't throw it off the road. A nice chap, too."

He would finish an impressive fifth in the final, Beckwith having retired in his heat. Van Lennep would be retained for the July 9 Coupe de Vitesse de l'AC Normandie contest, which supported the Rouen Grand Prix Formula Two round, finishing an eventual eleventh, and penultimate finisher, on aggregate, while Beckwith recorded another DNF after his car's Variomatic transmission failed. The duo remained in France for the following weekend's Grand Prix de la Ville de Nevers race in Magny-Cours, where the DAFs had no answer to the front running Matras of Henri Pescarolo or Jean-Pierre Jaussaud, but van Lennep managed to finish third in his heat before placing fifth in the final, sandwiched by the Alpines of François Cevert and Patrick Depailler. Beckwith's poor luck continued as further mechanical maladies restricted him to fifteenth place.

There then followed a much-needed hiatus before a return visit to The Netherlands for the August 27 Zandvoort Trophy Formula Three race. Beckwith was fastest aboard his DAF, now running a Ford engine prepared by Charles Lucas Engineering, and he led the first of the 24 race laps ahead of Roy Pike, Clay Regazzoni and John Miles. The lead quartet chopped and changed places until the ninth tour, when Beckwith spun with fourth-place man Regazzoni rotating in sympathy. Meanwhile, the sister car of van Lennep was already out with an electrical problem. In a race that witnessed several cars suffer fuel starvation, or pirouette on an increasingly slippery circuit, it was left to the works Matras of Henri Pescarolo and Jean-Pierre Jaussaud to emerge victorious. Beckwith, who was running on Dunlop wet weather tyres, came home an eventual fifth. A weekend later, the 'Flag would return behind the Iron Curtain to contest the Formula Three Brno Grand Prix in Czechoslovakia. Both Beckwith and van Lennep lapped the Masaryk circuit below the existing lap record to line up on the front row alongside the de Sanctis of Manfred Mohr. The lead trio battled hard for the opening laps but, as the race progressed, van Lennep was forced to retire his DAF with a split fuel tank. Battle raged between Beckwith and Mohr until two laps from the end when the exhaust fell off the Briton's car, his German rival leading him home by 12 seconds following more than an hour's racing.

By comparison, the September 17 Coupe de l'Avenir contest at Zolder witnessed a poor showing, with Beckwith and Van Lennep finishing seventh and eighth on aggregate. However, at the Swedish Skarpnäcks circuit on September 24, the Formula Three race was dominated by the Anglo-Dutch pairing, with Beckwith a late retirement thanks to a broken tappet, leaving van Lennep a clear run to victory ahead of Lars Lindberg and Ronnie Peterson. The 'Flag and DAF then rounded out the season – and their relationship – with a heated Formula Three contest at the Jarama circuit in Spain on November 12, with Beckwith finishing third on aggregate behind Regazzoni and Reine Wissell, with van Lennep sixth.

While not a banner year for the 'Flag, there had been successes, and with a car of its own construction. However, as the curtain came down on the '67 season, Warner's team faced an uncertain future.

IX. Music, maestro, please!

If motorsport teaches you one thing over the long run, it's pragmatism. After the team's trade support dried up at the end of 1966, Warner had wisely concluded that funding a single-seater campaign was prohibitive, and he was no longer prepared to dig deep into his own pocket. The 'Flag's deal with DAF ensured that the manufacturer underwrote the programme, but with that arrangement amicably terminated at the end of '67, options for the new season appeared bleak. Warner, however, was about to pull off a coup that would ensure the team's continued presence in Formula Three.

The 'Flag attracted sponsorship from Scalextric for its 1968 Formula Three campaign with a pair of quasi-works McLarens.

Mike Walker was employed as lead driver in the 'Flag's F3 team, and would win during the 1968 season.

"We were promised trade backing for the year and that would be in the form of bonuses," Warner recalls. "However, to receive a bonus we not only had to win, but we had to win at International level. Overt sponsorship at that time was completely unknown in Europe, but I had been investigating potential sponsors away from the usual fuel, oil, and tyre companies. While that was going on, I was approached by Bruce McLaren to look after the works Formula Two team for '68. Bruce was a lovely guy, and we reached a deal whereby I would run Robin Widdows – who had previously driven for us on occasion – in the lead M4A. The sister car would be driven by Graeme Lawrence, a Kiwi who Bruce rated highly.

"On top of that, we reached an agreement for the 'Flag to enter two McLaren Formula Three cars on a quasi-works basis. I managed to get Triang, which made Scalextric slot-cars, to back us, and it put up £5000. They didn't want to help with the parallel Formula Two team, but they insisted that our F3 drivers should look the part. They wanted to promote a young, clean-cut image and asked for photos of our proposed drivers. Fortunately, they were happy with our choices of Mike Walker and Ian Ashley. We then put on a big press 'do' in February '68 with two cars decked out

Teenage up-and-comer Ian Ashley would drive the second F3 McLaren in his first full season of international motorsport.

with Scalextric logos: this was a few months before Gold Leaf colours first appeared on a Grand Prix Lotus. We would run the works cars as the Chequered Flag-McLaren Racing Team, and Mike and Ian under the Chequered Flag-Scalextric Racing Team banner."

Team leader Widdows had shown form in Formula Two the previous year aboard his own Witley Racing Syndicate Brabham, while Lawrence arrived in Europe fresh from impressing at national level. The Formula Three squad similarly mixed a blend of youth and experience, Walker having emerged from the '67 season as *Autosport*'s 'most improved driver' while 19-year-old Ashley had marked himself out as a press-

on driver in a Merlyn Mk10. For Walker in particular, it was a dream seat. "I had driven with Frank Manning that year and at the end of the season I was contacted by Rodney Bloor: would I be interested in driving for his Sports Motors team in '68?" he recalls. "I was, but around the same time Graham approached me with a view to driving his number one car in Formula Three. It would be mostly on the International scene, which was exactly what I wanted. Graham had run several drivers who I admired, such as Roy Pike and Chris Irwin, and had ambitious plans for the future. He offered me a £1000 retainer and a percentage of any prize money, so obviously I was tempted, but I told him that I would

Warner's trip to the Barcelona Grand Prix meeting at Montjuïc Park involved a detour to buy this Pontiac GTO convertible. High jinks ensued …

have to speak to Rodney first. Rodney told me I had to drive for Graham as it was such a great opportunity. The Chequered Flag really was the team which you aspired to drive for, so I signed with Graham. I was over the moon."

As was Ashley. "Graham was like a kind and concerned uncle to me. He and his wife Shirley were very welcoming and generous. I first met Graham at the daunting Charade circuit at Clermont-Ferrand before my maiden big International F3 race in 1967. Graham introduced himself and was very encouraging. We kept in touch throughout that year and he generously paid for my Merlyn's engine to be rebuilt and uprated by Charles Lucas Engineering towards the end of the season. I had the offer of a works Merlyn F3 drive for '68 alongside Tony Lanfranchi, and Natalie Goodwin was also keen to run me in her F3 team, but the opportunity to drive for the famous and very successful Chequered Flag team was a dream come true."

The season kicked off on March 31 with the Barcelona Grand Prix meeting at Montjuïc Park. For Walker the flight to Spain would prove an eye-opener. "Graham suggested we meet up at Heathrow and fly out together. I got to the airport and then Graham mentioned that we would fly to Madrid first before driving to Barcelona; he had some business to attend to before the races. In those days there were no X-ray machines or suchlike at airports, you just had to produce your passport. Well, we walked up to passport control and Graham motioned for me to go first. I presented my passport and, as I stepped through the counter area, Graham nonchalantly passed me his briefcase while he rooted around for his passport. We then went through to the duty free area and waited for the flight to be called. Graham then said rather casually: 'I'd better take that off you'. At that time the Harold Wilson government had limited the amount of money you could take out of the country to just £50, and on the flight over I learned that the briefcase contained about £2500! The word 'cool' gets bandied around a lot, but Graham really was one cool customer!"

"The money was for a fully-loaded Pontiac GTO convertible," Warner recalls. "It had been left in the airport car park by its owner who had been posted to Vietnam. I had to pay a huge parking charge only to then discover that all the tyres were bald – despite there being only 5000 miles on clock! But that thing would lay down big black streaks of rubber without even trying. While we were in Barcelona, I went out for dinner with Colin Chapman, Jimmy Clark and Graham Hill. They encouraged a hilarious ride back to the hotel and, even at modest speed, I spun the car on damp cobbles and sailed backwards into a parking slot right outside the hotel entrance!"

By contrast, enjoyment was in short supply trackside. The works McLarens had been completed mere days before the event so they arrived in Spain without the benefit of a shakedown. As Jackie Stewart emerged victorious in the Formula Two encounter, Widdows finished a lapped seventh. Lawrence, who had been demonstrably slower than his team-mate in practice, failed to finish. Walker managed to salvage some glory for the 'Flag with pole position for the opening Formula Three heat, which he led then for ten laps, only to spin off after the engine seized. His team-mate fared even worse. "My car wouldn't even start so I didn't qualify," Ashley recalls.

For Warner, the team's next outing would be tinged with sorrow. On the fifth lap of the Deutschland Trophy race at Hockenheim on April 7, his good friend Jim Clark perished after crashing his Lotus 48. "The circuit was damp and on a fast but gentle right-hand bend, Jimmy's car left the road and struck a tree. Colin Chapman wasn't at the race so I had the traumatic task of breaking the news of Jimmy's death to his team-mate Graham Hill, who was sitting in the front of the Team Lotus transporter. It was just awful. I had breakfasted with a downcast Jimmy that morning and we were joined at the table by Ashley, who idolised Jimmy. Everyone did. Jimmy didn't like the circuit or the dismal weather and told us his Lotus had been plagued by a slight but intermittent misfire during practice. As it happens, Widdows had been only a few car lengths behind when Jimmy went off. Robin finished eighth on aggregate but Lawrence wasn't classified. Not that anyone really cared about results that day."

Ashley's car suffered another mystery engine ailment on April 12 for round four of the BRSCC Trophy series at Oulton Park, which also had International status. "We towed it around but it just wouldn't run," he recalls. Walker, by contrast, claimed victory on aggregate ahead of Tony Lanfranchi. Three days later, the team was at Thruxton for the Easter Monday Formula Two race, Widdows retiring his car from the second heat with a fractured fuel pipe with Lawrence coming home thirteenth in the final. The équipe then headed for France and the April 21 Grand Prix de Ville de Pau. Widdows qualified sixth, his team-mate ending up almost seven seconds per-lap slower. After Jochen Rindt was knocked out following a minor incident, Jackie Stewart was untroubled up front, but in the closing stages all eyes were on the battle for second place. Jean-Pierre Beltoise was eager to make it a Matra one-two finish, but Widdows fended him off for the final 15 of 70 laps to come home runner-up by a whisker. Lawrence was classified ninth, five laps in arrears. In the Formula Three support race, Ashley finally managed his maiden start – and finish – of the

Mike Walker (blue jacket) in conversation with multiple F3 champion Harry Stiller at Oulton Park in April 1968. Walker would take his first win for the 'Flag at this meeting. (Courtesy Simon Scott)

Walker leads Peter Gethin (Chevron, left) and Charles Lucas (Titan, far left) out of Lodge Corner en route to victory at Oulton Park in April 1968. (Courtesy Simon Scott)

'68 season in seventh place, as Walker retired his car with gear-selection problems.

It was back to native soil for the Scalextric squad's next outing, Walker finishing fifth in the April 27 BRDC Caravans International Trophy race at Silverstone, with Ashley an embattled fourteenth. A day later, Widdows retired from the Madrid Grand Prix at Jarama while his team-mate failed to even qualify. The following weekend, he would finish twelfth in the Limbourg Grand Prix at Zolder, Belgium, as Widdows placed sixth, leaving Warner and Bruce McLaren to ponder Lawrence's future with the team. *Motor Racing* magazine was particularly scornful, its end-of-year review stating haughtily: "What a mistake Lawrence was! Firstly he should never have been allowed into a works F2 car, and secondly certain key people failed to realise that the national single-seater class in Australia and New Zealand is in fact little more than a club affair, even though on paper it looks pretty serious."

Lawrence was dropped on his return from Belgium, his failure to get up to speed proving a mystery to Warner: "He clearly had ability, and Bruce thought he had something after his performances in the Tasman series, but he was consistently slower than Widdows by several seconds. The F2 McLaren wasn't brilliant, and I think Robin was a lot better than he was ever given credit for. To some degree he simply drove around the M4A's flaws, but Lawrence didn't seem to have that in him. We ended up replacing him with Frank Gardner, who was a good development driver and an experienced racer. That

The underrated Rob Widdows was de facto leader of the F2 team ...

... here, he fends off a determined Jean-Pierre Beltoise to finish second to Jackie Stewart at Pau in April 1968.

said, I never believed Frank was quite as good as he thought he was."

If the Formula Two programme wasn't quite living up to expectations, the 'Flag's Formula Three bid was similarly failing to find traction. A run at Montlhéry near Paris on May 12 ended with Walker's car catching fire, with Ashley coming in a down-on-power twelfth. "The McLaren wasn't a great car," Walker says. "1968 was the year of the Tecno chassis and the Firestone YB11 tyre. If you had both, you had the hot ticket. Our car, by comparison, was more difficult to drive and lacked the development input needed to make it really competitive."

The season was about to get a whole lot worse. The 'Flag returned to Monaco for the May 25 Formula Three race that supported the Formula One World Championship round. Walker was one of the fastest men on track in qualifying, "Then I made a mistake at the chicane and made a mess of the McLaren against the Armco along the front of the harbour. It was the same spot where Paul Hawkins had famously gone into the water a few years earlier. I apologised to Graham, who was always very good in such a situation. After we had recovered the car, he said the best thing we could do now was to go and have breakfast, which is exactly what we did …"

An embattled Ashley, meanwhile, didn't make the final. The Monaco curse had struck again, but Warner had more pressing problems. "I wasn't so much worried about the bent car. We had built our own chassis jigs and made body moulds after all. We ended up making more monocoques than McLaren itself, but in the run up to Monaco I'd learned that we were losing our trade backing. Esso in particular had dramatically shrunk its motorsport budget and that was a real bombshell."

The Formula Two campaign continued apace at Crystal Palace on June 3, with both works cars having been rebuilt and modified with repositioned suspension pick-up points. New incumbent Gardner belied his lack of seat time to comfortably make the cut for the London Trophy as Widdows suffered a miserable qualifying session, first with an overheating engine, and later with a snapped throttle cable. However, in the opening heat he made a splendid start from the fourth row of the grid, while Gardner's race ended on the twelfth lap with electrical issues. Widdows came home fourth only to glance the barriers at Park Curve in the final after running out of road while in seventh place. Matters didn't improve in the Rhine Cup Formula Two round at Hockenheim a fortnight later. Gardner impressed with a fine qualifying effort to line up fifth on the grid and gamely clung on to the lead battle during the opening heat, only to retire the car on the twelfth lap with falling oil pressure. Widdows, meanwhile, was embroiled in an epic battle with Jonathan Williams, despite a failing clutch. He then spun off at half-distance and was unable to restart the ailing McLaren.

The Scalextric team was one man short for the Guards International Trophy meeting at Oulton Park on June 23, Ashley claiming sixth place on aggregate. Walker's absence from the sister car was due to him competing in the Monza Lottery Formula Two race that same weekend. "Frank Gardner was unable to drive at Monza due to other commitments. Graham was obviously disappointed with how the season was panning out for both the team and me. He asked if I would like to step up to the F2 car for Monza and I immediately said yes. That would be my first drive of an F2 car and visit to Monza. The race for the Gran Premio Della Lotteria was to be run over 45 laps, and by lap 22 the leading group, of which I was one – having qualified 12th out of 22 starters – was running close together. Then, coming out of the Parabolica, Derek Bell triggered an almighty pile-up in his Ferrari. Seven cars were eliminated. Fortunately, I came through the melee without serious damage to the car, needing only to change a wheel. I was able to finish the race, albeit in eleventh place. Jonathan Williams won from Alan Rees with my team-mate Robin finishing third."

Walker would return to Formula Three for the Coupe de Vitesse meeting at Rouen on July 14, placing a fine fourth overall on aggregate. His team-mate, however, went off in the biggest way possible in practice, as Warner recalls: "Ian came past us at an almighty clip and went off on the right-hand bend just after the pits, and ended up inverted in a concrete drainage ditch. It happened right in front of Bruce McLaren and Denny Hulme …"

Ashley recalls: "That was the second lap of practice, and my second ever lap of the circuit. I came past the pits with a jammed throttle, the return-spring having broken. Graham found it dangling free later on."

Gardner reclaimed his seat for the next round of the European Formula Two Championship at Langenlebarn, Austria on July 14. As Jochen Rindt claimed his second consecutive victory on home soil, the 'Flag had another weekend to forget. Widdows was running fifth in the opening heat, only to clout a hay bale which prompted a visit to the pits. The car returned trackside with a slipping clutch and wasn't classified in the final order. Gardner, meanwhile, rounded out his brief stint with the team with ninth place on aggregate. The Scalextric team, meanwhile, rounded out with Walker and Ashley both recording DNFs in the Clearways Trophy encounter at Brands Hatch on July 20, the lone entry for Ashley at the AMOC Martini Trophy meeting at Silverstone a week

Australian all-rounder Frank Gardner replaced the uncompetitive Graeme Lawrence in the F2 squad partway through the 1968 season.

later being scratched due to problems with the car. Gardner had now vacated his Formula Two car, with Walker being reinstated for the Grand Prix of Zandvoort on July 28 alongside team leader Widdows.

The meeting would be marred by tragedy after Chris Lambert crashed fatally after his Brabham was struck by Clay Regazzoni's Tecno in the final. Walker had retired from the first heat following a spin, with Widdows claiming an eventual sixth place. The Formula Two McLaren clearly wasn't a frontrunner but, for the following round at Enna on August 25, the team conceived a new aerofoil to be mounted directly behind the driver's head. However, a slight discrepancy in measurement meant that they wouldn't fit either car, the boss having brought them over to Sicily as hand luggage! Both McLarens were plagued with fuel pump issues, with Walker retiring and Widdows being classified fourteenth and last.

The cash-strapped Formula Three squad, meanwhile, showed well in the Zandvoort Trophy meeting the following weekend, with Ashley holding an impressive sixth place for most of the race. As Justin Haler reported in *Autosport*: "[He] was driving the race of his life. Some way past the halfway stage, he noticed the handling was somewhat odd and put it down to his driving, but little did he know that he had run over a piece of debris and that a tyre was slowly deflating."

Music, maestro, please!

Walker (wearing borrowed helmet) retired from fourth place in the Clearways Trophy race at Brands Hatch in July 1968.

Ashley managed to hold on for a further six laps to come home seventh. However the writing was on the wall, and writ large. The Formula Three adventure came to an end on September 2 at Brands Hatch, Walker crashing out of his heat with Ashley retiring his car from the final with an oil leak.

The Formula Two squad's days were also up. Widdows vacated the team ahead of the September 15 Grand Prix de Reims, ending his year driving a David Bridges Racing Lola T100. Walker, meanwhile, was unclassified in the final order and saw out the season driving a works Merlyn Mk12. The team was quietly disbanded, the 'Flag concentrating instead on selling cars rather than racing them. "It was an incredibly sad time for all of us," Warner recalls. "Motorsport was changing. You could have the best car one weekend but you could be a complete also-ran next time out as something new had come along. I had to be pragmatic: there was no way that I could personally fund programmes in Formula Three or suchlike. Also, I wasn't willing to endanger the core business."

In a bid to distance himself from motor racing, Warner instead set about exploring another great passion as a business activity. As the '60s drew to a close, he would become a music mogul. "Music has always had a considerable influence on my life," he says. "I have enjoyed, or been involved with, many different forms of music at various stages of my life. When I was a small child, my father had a wind-up gramophone and a few 78rpm records. My brothers and I played them hundreds of times. I also sang in the All Hallows church choir, and although I cannot now sing in tune at all, I could then and was lucky to have a fine treble voice. I sang solos for visiting bishops and at several carol services. I became head chorister, which lasted until my voice broke. I was also in the school choir, and we put on Handel's Messiah a couple of times.

"By the time I joined the RAF, I gained much pleasure from listening to what is now termed classical music and built up a collection of 78s, and then long-playing records. During my 18-month pilot's course at 4 FTS Heany, near Bulawayo in Southern Rhodesia, I took over the Station Music Circle from a cadet who had completed his course, received his Wings and been posted back to the UK. That gave me access to a large collection of classical records, and I put on a weekly evening concert of recordings in a lecture room, selecting the pieces to be played and writing the programme notes, so I had to 'gen up' on the composers, their lives and their works. These notes were designed to make the music less highbrow and more accessible. This aim was achieved as the weekly attendance grew, including officers, ground crew and other station personnel, as well as aircrew cadets.

"Back in the UK, I went to as many concerts as possible while on leave from the RAF, including many proms. I would go by public transport from home in Whitton, joining the long queue at the back of the Albert Hall, and when I started going out with my future wife Shirley, I took her to several concerts. However, she preferred romantic singers such as Johnny Mathis, Nat King Cole, and Frank Sinatra. I grew to like this kind of music, too, and we went to see them all, plus performances by Ray Charles, Sammy Davis and Ella Fitzgerald. These broadened my musical horizons. We also went to Humphrey Littleton's Jazz Club in Oxford Street several times, and later to Ronnie Scott's club to see John Dankworth and Cleo Lane, Oscar Peterson and the like. Then The Beatles burst upon the scene. Following some lively singles, they released their iconic album *Sgt Pepper's Lonely Hearts Club Band* which changed popular music forever. It became an all-time favourite of mine alongside Pink Floyd's wonderful *Dark Side of the Moon*."

The move from listener to record label owner was prompted by a former 'Flag salesman. "A rather forceful character who had worked for us had gone into the music agency business, booking bands into universities under the alias Marc Newton – he was called Caldwell Smythe during his 'Flag days. He talked me into starting an agency with Lee Allen and Del Taylor, two well-connected bookers he worked with. The move was encouraged by one of their leading artists, Alexis Korner, who was a big name at the centre of most of the period's major bands. He was a great performer but also a key facilitator and a super chap. He, Lee,

Marc, and Del assured me that they could break away cleanly from their current agency as they were owed commission, so we formed Planned Entertainments. We placed full-page adverts in *Melody Maker*, which included my name as well as theirs."

Then it all began to unravel. "Shortly thereafter, while on holiday with Shirley and her mother Edna at our villa in Spain, I received ever-more frantic phone calls – Planned Entertainment had been served with a series of High Court writs by the owner of [my partners'] previous agency, a rather furious Greek character. He alleged breach of contract and wanted a vast sum in damages. He also applied for an injunction to force PE to cease trading immediately. Unfortunately, my partners were impecunious so it all fell on me – any one partner is liable for the actions of any other – and we had to defend a separate action against Alexis as an artist, too. I instructed leading solicitors Harbottle & Lewis, and we negotiated an out-of-court settlement. It cost me hundreds of pounds each month for five years, and I had to pay the legal fees of both parties. It was an expensive lesson!"

Nonetheless, he persisted with the venture. "I had rented a large flat next to the 'Flag showrooms which PE used as a suite of offices, and we struggled on booking groups. Unfortunately, there was a clash of egos between my partners. We almost merged with First Class Agency, which was run by Barry Class, but I called it off as I thought we would likely end up being turned over. Lee then tried to get me to take over the management of The Foundations, a soul band which had enjoyed a number one hit with *Baby Now That I've Found You*, but they were too large, fractious and costly to run. They were always bickering, so I left them well alone. Thus Planned Entertainment morphed into Delta Artists Management. That was just Del Taylor, the most sensible of our bookers, and I, plus office staff. We then took new offices at the Hammersmith end of Chiswick High Road. Del, helped by Alexis, put together several promising groups which Delta managed, including Warm Dust, Bandit and Liar. We arranged record deals for them and their albums and gigs received good reviews. We nearly got them to break into the all-important American market, and took offices in Sunset Boulevard, Los Angeles, to do just that. Our producer, John Alcock, who produced albums for Thin Lizzy, also lived in LA. Both Del and I made many trips there.

"Unfortunately, the record label we were signed to was part of the huge Warner Brothers empire, and the head of our label had been embroiled in an affair with the lead singer of one of Warner Bros' major acts. Before long, and in typical American style, they were busy suing one another. Although not involved directly in this, all groups on the label were barred from recording studios owned by Warner Bros. We had a group staying in an expensive hotel, a part-recorded album that we couldn't gain access to, outstanding studio fees and no way forward – so that was the end of Delta Artists Management."

Warner's flirtation with the music business had proved a costly one. It had been an intriguing diversion, but the lure of motorsport was never far away. The 1970s would witness a return of the Chequered Flag name to the headlines, but in an entirely new arena.

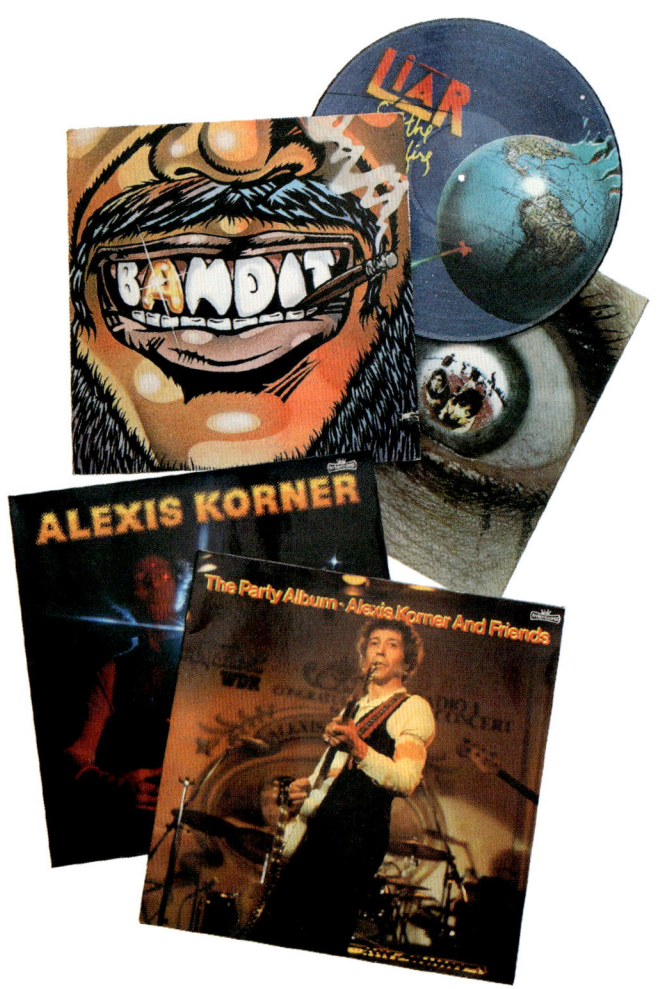

Following his withdrawal from motorsport, Warner explored his other great passion and became a music mogul. Blues legend Alexis Korner became a great friend and close ally in the music business.

X. Rallying cry

The early 1970s weren't kind to the motor trade. A credit squeeze allied to the arrival of VAT, the three-day working week, and a fuel crisis all served to affect The Chequered Flag's core business. Having spent an estimated £500,000 on motorsport during the previous decade, the boss had no intention of spending more, but that was before one of his former drivers began twisting arms and calling-in favours. The 'Flag was heading for Formula One – sort of.

Warner recalls: "It was Ian Ashley's doing. He was incredibly keen, and you couldn't help but be swept up by his enthusiasm. He desperately wanted to become a Grand Prix driver and badgered me constantly: would I help him? His '68 season hadn't gone well, what with the big shunt at Rouen and so on, but at times he had been bloody quick. I'd watched him develop as a driver and was aware that he'd won quite a few races in Formula 5000. That made me think, 'Well, if he can handle one of those things, he

Ray Mallock attends to his Ensign's rear wing. The Chequered Flag sponsored him in Formula Atlantic in 1974.

must be good enough for F1'. I had no intention of actually running him in a car though.

"By this point the 'Flag had been out of motor racing for quite a while, although we did sponsor Russell Wood during the 1973 Formula Three season. He was quite a handy driver who went well in a March 733, but we never owned the car. We also backed Ray Mallock in Formula Atlantic in '74, but I wasn't interested in becoming an entrant. The thing is, Ian was persistent. He kept chipping away, which led to me getting embroiled in the Token F1 project."

The Token RJ02 was an honest workmanlike machine, comprising a slender monocoque, Cosworth DFV engine, and Hewland FGA400 'box. Designer Ray Jessop installed Tom Pryce for its maiden race at the April 7 BRDC International Trophy meeting at Silverstone. He managed only three laps in practice and 15 laps of the race before retiring the car with gear-linkage failure. The Welshman debuted the car at World Championship level in the Belgian Grand Prix only to depart for the UOP Shadow team shortly thereafter, while the preternaturally brave Dave Purley failed to qualify for the British Grand Prix. Then it was Ashley's turn.

He recalls: "In August '74 I had just finished an F5000 race at Brands Hatch driving for Jackie Epstein's ShellSport/Radio-Luxemburg team when someone from Token approached my friend and manager, Mike Smith, about a possible drive in the Token for the German Grand Prix. Following a brief natter with Graham Warner and [oil trader] Richard Oaten, I agreed to do it so long as I could have a quick test at Goodwood first. On the Tuesday before the race, I did maybe twelve laps.

"At the Nürburgring, the right-front tyre went flat at the bottom of the Foxhole on the third lap of practice. In second practice, a mechanic effectively foiled my efforts as he had mistakenly installed the wrong top gear so instead of having 11,000rpm, I had only 9000. We qualified, but for the warm-up lap Jessop told me to be careful and lift-off at the Foxhole, what with all the extra race fuel onboard. I did just that but the right-front tyre blew again at precisely the same spot. I continued on for another 10 miles, arriving at the pits without the tyre and the right-front wing. Ray was concerned that vibrations may have cracked the top front wishbone so he changed it in record time, eyeballing the camber and toe-in settings. There was no replacement wing so they simply taped up the wing support to keep it in place, increased left-front wing and reduced the rear wing. Ray then wished me luck.

"I remember Jackie Stewart sauntering along the grid. When he finally arrived at my car, he looked at the somewhat excessive right-hand camber/toe-in and the bandaged right wing pole, then shook his head and smiled!"

Ashley finished fourteenth following another identical front-right puncture, the issue in time being traced to a batch of porous wheels. "For the next race, the Austrian GP at the Ostereichering, there was only the one flat tyre, this time the left-front. I was doing 180mph-plus at the end of the pit straight heading into the flat out right-hander at the time. In the race, a left-front tyre began bubbling: the glassfibre front

The Chequered Flag stepped up to Formula One in 1974 on acquiring an ex-John Watson Brabham BT42. It would prove a costly – and fruitless – campaign.

wings were flexing at high speed and this reduced front-left grip and overheated the inside tread. Ray then called me in for another lightening two minute pit stop. Then my left-rear wheel came loose. In I came again but while they replaced it the engine began to overheat. They thought the car was on fire so hauled me out only to realise it was just steam. I clambered back in and off I went to finish eight laps down on the winner, Carlos Reutemann."

Warner was by now exasperated. "We were clearly on a hiding to nothing with Token. I'd had enough, and did a deal with the Hexagon team to buy the Brabham BT42 in which John Watson had started the '74 season. I thought I was buying an on-the-button, ready to go Formula One car, but it was delivered in bits – and the early bits, too, as none of the later development parts were included."

Ashley's loyalties were also about to be tested: "Graham and Richard were pretty pissed off with Token which led to them buying the Brabham. John Surtees then phoned and invited me to Goodwood to test his car. Finally starting at 4pm, I did one lap before returning on seven cylinders. They checked a couple of things and I went out again, only to come back in almost immediately. Without proper power the car just understeered. Afterwards they asked me what I thought. I'd just had a belly-full of this with Token but I was diplomatic!

"'Well, you've got the drive,' Surtees said the following day. 'You can finish the season – Monza, Mosport and Watkins Glen.' I asked for two days to decide, since I was contractually tied with Epstein for F5000. I didn't know what to say to Graham who'd purchased the darn Brabham with some help from Richard. The Brabham was potentially a good car so I phoned Surtees and declined his offer. He wasn't impressed! The Brabham we'd been sold was a total bitsa, though, and I failed to qualify for the Canadian or the US Grands Prix. Just to rub salt into the wounds, when I arrived at Watkins Glen I was greeted with the news that my father had been killed. In hindsight, I probably should have accepted the Surtees drive, but then the fellow who took it, Helmuth Koinnigg, had brake failure at the 'Glen, crashed through the Armco and was decapitated. There but for the grace of God …"

For Warner, the Grand Prix adventure was over. "It was a complete waste of money. We gained nothing

Graham Warner overcame his dislike of rallying to field the most instantly recognisable cars in 1970s British national rallying.

The Chequered Flag became concessionaire for the Brazilian Puma marque in 1974, only to have to withdraw from the UK market under pressure from Ford, which claimed ownership of the name.

from doing it." On a similar note, earlier in the year he had taken a stand at the Racing Car Show at Olympia. The 'Flag had become the UK concessionaire for the Brazilian Puma marque and displayed a GTE coupé which was on sale for £2198. "That all came about via Emerson Fittipaldi. The cars were made in his home town, Sao Paulo, and he made some introductions. It was a glassfibre-bodied car with a very professional level of fit and finish. It went well with a tuned VW engine, too. We planned to import the GTE and the open-top Spyder version, and went so far as to have an actual Puma – in a cage of course – on the stand. However, the organisers didn't take kindly to that, so it was removed pretty quickly. Then Ford stamped on us: we were informed that it had rights to the Puma name so we only ever imported the one car. Of course, it took more than two decades before Ford introduced a car in Europe with the Puma name …"

Down but not out, Warner changed tack and ventured off-piste. "It was PR man Richard Banks who talked me into rallying," he recalls. "My opinion on the sport had been coloured somewhat by my Monte adventure all those years ago. Richard did his best to persuade me that it would be good publicity for us if we got involved, but I wasn't convinced. I begrudgingly agreed to go with him to watch the RAC Rally in November 1974 and came away impressed by how the sport had progressed. I thought, 'Blimey, these guys don't hang about', but I knew that if we were going to do it, we had to make an impact."

Having taken on a Lancia concession in the early '70s, Warner's thoughts naturally turned to fielding a Stratos, the Dino V6-engined supercar pinup which had turned rallying on its head that decade. "We sold more Lancias than any other dealer in the UK and obviously I thought it would be good to be seen running a Lancia rather than something like a Ford Escort. However, Lancia UK thought otherwise. We were told that if we went rallying with a Stratos, we'd only do harm to the name. This was at a time when they sponsored the Lancia Trophy for eventing. I argued that we sold Lancias, not horses, but we had to jump over a lot of hurdles.

"The factory didn't want to know either – quite the opposite. It was Mike Parkes who made all the difference. I'd known Mike since he'd raced Geminis for us, and he was responsible for turning the standard Stratos into something fit for rallying. Through him we got an entrée to Lancia's competition chief Cesare Fiorio. To begin with it was all, 'No, no, no,' but eventually we got him to sell us a crashed one."

Three Lancias had gone off on the same corner on the Monte Carlo Rally in January 1975, and Warner bought the ex-Pinto/Andruet car. "Of course we had to pay cost! We straightened it out, got it going, but we only had one spare engine. We needed it almost straight away, too. The factory neglected to mention that it had removed the oil cooler, and there was merely a heat exchanger. As soon as we went testing in Sweden the oil overheated and the engine blew!

"We had good drivers, though. Initially we had Per-Inge Walfridsson who was outstanding on the loose stuff, and Cahal 'CB' Curley from Ireland who was brilliant on Tarmac. He was a hero in his homeland; they sang songs about him. On our first event, the March 27-April 4 1975 Circuit of Ireland, people were actually singing his name as we walked along!" Nonetheless, Curley and co-driver Austin Frazer didn't make it past the third stage – the team had packed a wealth of parts, but they didn't stretch to a spare engine.

While the Chequered Flag Stratos racked up more than its fair share of column inches in the specialist press, it wasn't always for the right reasons. On the next event, May's Welsh International Rally, Walfridsson starred during the early running, only for the car's oil pressure to drop suddenly. Rather than risk another expensive blow up, the Swede coasted to the end of the Pantperthog stage and into retirement. A month later, Walfridsson and co-driver John Jensen went fastest on four of the first five stages, only to retire from a 20 second lead with a terminal loss of transmission fluid. At the end of June, Cahal was back in for the Donegal International Rally. Unfortunately, his run was effectively over on the opening stage after the Stratos connected with a bridge parapet. Warner recalls: "We had to take – borrow, rather – an upright from a spectator's Fiat 127 in the car park. We asked the owner and he said, 'For CB? Oh yes!'"

However, on stage five, Crocknakilla, the replacement item collapsed, resulting in another DNF.

With Walfridsson reinstated for the August '75 Burmah Rally, the misbehaving Lancia's engine cover was up at the end of the first stage. The 'Flag mechanics managed to get it going again, only for the car to retire with broken rear suspension after the Stratos smacked a large rock. It wasn't until October '75 that it finally lasted the distance, when new incumbent Tony Pond brought the car home third on the Castrol event – minus four working gears.

"It was an uphill battle," Warner admits. "We were often the quickest guys out there. We'd set fastest

Tony Pond and co-driver David Richards claimed a maiden finish for the team's Stratos with third place on the October 1975 Castrol 75 rally.

stage times, but we had a lot of retirements. The problem was we had no support. If Lancia had let us have bits as they became available rather than us having to beg for them, it would have helped immeasurably. On one occasion we purchased a lot of spares from the factory. A short while later we received a supplementary invoice for millions of lira, increasing the price of parts retrospectively. That was typical."

There was, however, a moment of glory for the team, and it wasn't with the Stratos. The 'Flag had hedged its bets and purchased a secondhand 3-litre Porsche 911 Carrera RSR for the princely sum of £9500. "That was prompted by Cahal," Warner recalls. "He had plenty of experience of Porsches and felt a 911 was the way to go for Tarmac rallies. We rallied the Stratos because it was a Lancia and we were Lancia dealers – it made sense to compete with what you were selling – but it was costing me a fortune. The Porsche, though, was solid as a rock. It was a proper works-spec car which we bought from the factory team via AFN. It couldn't have been a smoother transaction. They had the car delivered on time, and for the price we had agreed, and even managed to find a few extra horsepower than originally promised. The difference between working with the Germans and the Italians was like night and day."

Curley debuted the Carrera on the mid-September Manx International Rally. Unfortunately, he and wingman Frazer lost six minutes and a sure-fire second place late in the rally after an ignition lead came loose following a hard landing. It also didn't help that a fractured oil pipe was spraying lubricant over the front brakes and tyres. The duo eventually came home fifth overall, the 'Flag also coming to the aid of eighth place finishers Brian Evans and John Davenport, whose Porsche had lurched onto its side during the tricky Creg-Ny-Baa stage and bent its suspension.

A month later, Curley was on epic form on the Cork 20 Rally, which had attracted 91 crews, ten of them armed with Porsches. The winner of this asphalt event was in doubt until the very end, with the Evans Carrera seemingly poised for honours on Irish soil only for the penultimate stage times to be annulled after another competitor went off and triggered a monumental traffic jam. That revised the times, with Curley and co-driver Frazer claiming the Chequered Flag's first-ever rally win.

A Chequered Life

However, it was business as usual with the Stratos, with retirement for Walfridsson on November's RAC Rally, the car being withdrawn with a chronic misfire due to a seized cam-follower. But while the team's maiden season in rallying hadn't been without incident, 1975 drew to a close amid much publicity as Grand Prix charger Tom Pryce joined the team for a one-off outing. The Welshman's attempt on the December 28 Tour of Epynt proved brief, but it also showcased the tragic star's fêted car control and devotion to his home crowd.

The policeman's son, who earlier that year had won the Race of Champions for the Shadow équipe, didn't take much persuasion to switch disciplines after being approached by David Richards. Future Prodrive founder Richards was born in the same village as Pryce (Ruthin), and was then a regular with the Chiswick squad. The Stratos was the perfect foil for the F1 up-and-comer to showcase his burgeoning talent. "It was all David's doing," Warner recalls. "He was a very good organiser, very good on logistics, and an excellent co-driver. He was keen to put Pryce in the car and see if he could adapt. He also said it would be good publicity for us. His rally wasn't without its problems, though."

However, first came a couple of tests: on the loose surface in Bagshot, and then some sodden asphalt at the Longcross facility in Chobham, Surrey.

Autosport magazine's Peter Newton, who accompanied Pryce as he got to grips with a rally car for the first time, wrote: "If Formula One drivers are all alike, they really are a breed apart. Tom's feel for the car is uncanny … Pryce's reactions are staggering, as indeed they would have to be to hold a Shadow in powerslides at comfortably over 100mph on dry Tarmac but this is something else again."

Unfortunately, the rally proper ended just ten miles into the first stage. Proceeding downhill towards Fourways Bridge, the Stratos got out of shape on some mud and clipped a wall, with only a small boulder stopping the Lancia from plunging into a river. Richards was rushed to hospital to have stiches for a gashed knee, which had impacted with the dashboard. He would admit 30 years later that it was the only injury he ever incurred during his lengthy motorsport career.

With Richards – and the car – patched up, they tackled the Esgair Daffydd stage just to put on a show for the wildly partisan crowd. Though unable to compete for an official placing in the results, Pryce threw the Lancia around with abandon: he was clearly

The 'Flag team hedged its bets by purchasing this Porsche for asphalt rallies.

Above and left: Formula One star Tom Pryce enjoyed his test in the Stratos ahead of the 1975 Tour of Epynt. Unfortunately, he was to come unstuck on the daunting Welsh stages early on in the rally itself.

relishing the opportunity. An animated Pryce later told *Autosport*'s Pete Lyons, "That was fantastic! You could do anything with that Stratos … If I get another chance to do some more rallying, I'll take it like a shot because I thoroughly enjoyed it."

Sadly, he never had that chance, Pryce perishing in a ghastly – and unnecessary – accident during the 1977 South African GP. He would, however, not be the last big name star to find his way into a Chequered Flag Stratos.

After a frustrating 1975 campaign which resulted in just one finish for the Stratos, Warner and his team were nonetheless guardedly optimistic ahead of the new season. However, it was business as usual on the January '76 ShellSport Dean Rally with new appointee Andy Dawson being co-driven by *Motor Sport*'s assistant editor, Clive Richardson. The duo went fastest over the opening stage, only for the gearbox to fail shortly thereafter. They lost ten minutes while it was fixed and came home in 24th place – but at least it was a finish.

Curley and Frazer, meanwhile, were back in the Porsche for the Gallway International Rally on the first weekend of February. They went fastest on two of the first day's eight stages, only to retire the car with driveshaft failure following a rash of punctures. Meanwhile, in Belgium, Pond and Richards appeared set for a podium finish on the Boucles de Spa aboard the Stratos, only to get caught out on an icy stage on the final night of the event. They clipped a tree, sheering off the car's nose and damaging the radiator in the process.

Better times were ahead, though, as the 'Flag realised the car's potential once and, seemingly, for all over the weekend of February 22-23 1976, as Dawson and Andy Marriott conquered the forests of Yorkshire on the Mintex International Rally. "Tony Pond was unable to do it, so we looked around. Dawson was alright, he pressed on," Warner says.

Dawson recalls: "Everyone thinks the Stratos was a really powerful car but it had no low-down grunt and wasn't as quick in a straight line as the Escorts. What it did have was fantastic traction exiting tight corners – it was great out of 90 degree bends, and that helped on the Mintex."

However, the win was only awarded after a flurry of protests over an alleged time-keeping error on one of the opening day's stages. Following a four hour-long stewards' meeting, the stage in question was scratched from the timesheets and the Lancia duo were declared the victors, just 14 seconds ahead of Ford Escort RS1800 pairing Russell Brookes/John Brown. *Motorsport News* heaped praise on the winners but not the event organisers, its report surmising: "… no one would deny that the Chequered Flag team deserved their win at the weekend, a victory which could well mark the turning point for the UK-based Lancia Stratos and hopefully increase help from Lancia themselves."

However, elation turned to frustration on the following month's Granite Rally where a hidden boulder on the Benachie stage caught out several big names, with Dawson/Marriott among them. "The Stratos suffered broken rear suspension, which was heart-breaking for the team which had worked tirelessly to make the car

handle more predictably but was still waiting for parts from the works team with which to build a 300bhp-spec engine. It was still making do with 220bhp. We never did get our hands on a 24-valve engine, either. We only ever ran the 12-valve units. It didn't help that Tony Pond put it up a tree on the Cheltenham Forest Rally a few weeks later," Warner recalls. The car was rebuilt by chief mechanic Ron Pellett and his crew in

Warner (right) smiles as Andrew Marriott douses Andy Dawson with champagne following their 1976 Mintex Rally victory.

just a fortnight. New modifications included a stiffened central monocoque, reworked by Central Motors of Kilburn, and more robust suspension components fabricated by Chas Beattie. Also armed with a new, more powerful Racing Services-built V6, the car was ready for the Circuit of Ireland classic held over the Easter weekend, even if the factory had once again reneged on their promises to supply freshly homologated parts, such as bigger brakes.

"To get the Stratos finished in time was a remarkable achievement," Warner says. "We put Walfridsson in the car and also ran the Porsche for

Team co-ordinator Brendan Neville inspects the burnt-out remains of the team's first Stratos following its fiery exit on the 1976 Welsh Rally.

Curley. Unfortunately, he didn't finish as the car broke its steering following an off, but Walfridsson came home fourth overall which confirmed that we were going somewhere."

Then disaster struck during the May 7-9 Welsh Rally. "Some lunatic had removed a directional arrow from a tree on the Brechfa stage. There was a long straight with a series of brows followed by fast, tightening bends. Walfridsson came honking over one of the brows, tried to save it, but the nose caught a bank and the car became a ball of fire. They were trapped inside and the co-driver, John Jensen, broke his sternum. He was unconscious and wouldn't have emerged alive had it not been for a couple of guys who pulled him out. The fact that this was a closed stage where spectating was banned, well, you draw your own conclusions … As if that wasn't enough, we had stuff nicked from our service van, including a set of Minilite wheels and tyres, so I don't remember the Welsh Rally with great fondness …"

However, there was some light amid the gloom, with Curley and co-driver Drexel Gillespie taking the Porsche to an outright win with three minutes to spare on May's Moto '76 Rally. However, glory turned to despair the following month as Curley's bid for a fourth Donegal Rally came unstuck after a broken wishbone and trailing arm ended his run.

Meanwhile, back in Chiswick, the boss was tearing his hair out in frustration as he attempted to replace the comprehensively destroyed Stratos. "There was no way we could repair it – there was nothing to repair – so we then went back to Fiorio and once again were told that no new cars were available. Instead, we heard about one that had been a team car used for a Safari Rally recce. It had been left in Kenya so we mounted an expedition to Africa. The car was now owned by an Indian gentleman, and most of the good bits had been removed – including the cylinder heads. It was sitting on Volvo wheels and was badly damaged so it was obvious why the works team had abandoned the car. We crated it up and were at the airport in Uganda when bullets started flying. It was the night of the Entebbe Raid, where Israeli special forces attempted to rescue hostages from a hijacked plane. On top of that, when we finally got the car home it was impounded by customs. They put a ridiculously high value on the car. I said, 'Just look at it!' The thing was a wreck."

The team mounted an expedition to Kenya to retrieve this ex-recce car which had been left behind by the works squad. Note the Volvo wheels!

On finally agreeing a more realistic duty, the car was released and reconstructed in-house. Bearing the legend 'Stratos 2' on its nose, Chassis 1637 made its first appearance in Chequered Flag colours on the September '76 Ulster Rally with new boy Billy Coleman managing only 30 minutes of seat time at the Longcross test track beforehand. The team also fielded the Porsche for Curley and Frazer who were hoping to make up for the disappointment of retiring from the Donegal Rally two months earlier. They did just that, moving up the order to win as the Ford threat dissipated. Coleman, meanwhile, belied his lack of experience of the Lancia to come home in seventh place alongside co-driver Peter Scott.

Later that month, the team headed for the Isle of Man for a two-pronged attack on the Manx Rally. Walfridsson, this time with Martin Holmes reading the pace notes, almost came unstuck on the opening stage, spinning the Stratos at Signpost Corner which also caught out top stars Roger Clark and Jimmy McRae. Curley and Frazer, meanwhile, led an army of Porsches in pursuit of Escort man Ari Vatanen. However, the likelihood of a strong finish for both entries was dashed on the thirteenth stage, Sartfield, when Walfridsson came unstuck on a narrow section of asphalt running through a farmyard and bent the rear suspension. It was left to Curley to uphold the team's honour, but all hope of catching the flying Vatanen ended late in the day when he was forced to limp the Carrera for four miles with a puncture. The pounding broke a rear damper which further slowed his progress. Nonetheless, CB still had enough time in hand over the Triumph TR7 of Pond/Richards to finish second overall – his fourth runner-up placing on this classic rally.

The team rounded out the year with a tilt at December's RAC Rally, Walfridsson and co-driver Frazer struggling to overcome a fractured oil pipe, a collapsed upright and a lack of available gears before the inevitable retirement. It was a sad end to the season, which had started so well with honours on the Mintex International Rally. However, with that one result alone the 'Flag had bested the works team – it had made the Stratos a winner in Great Britain.

Above and right: The reconfigured car bears the legend 'Stratos 2' on its nose. 'Flag cars only ever ran 12-valve engines as the factory wouldn't release a 24-valve unit.

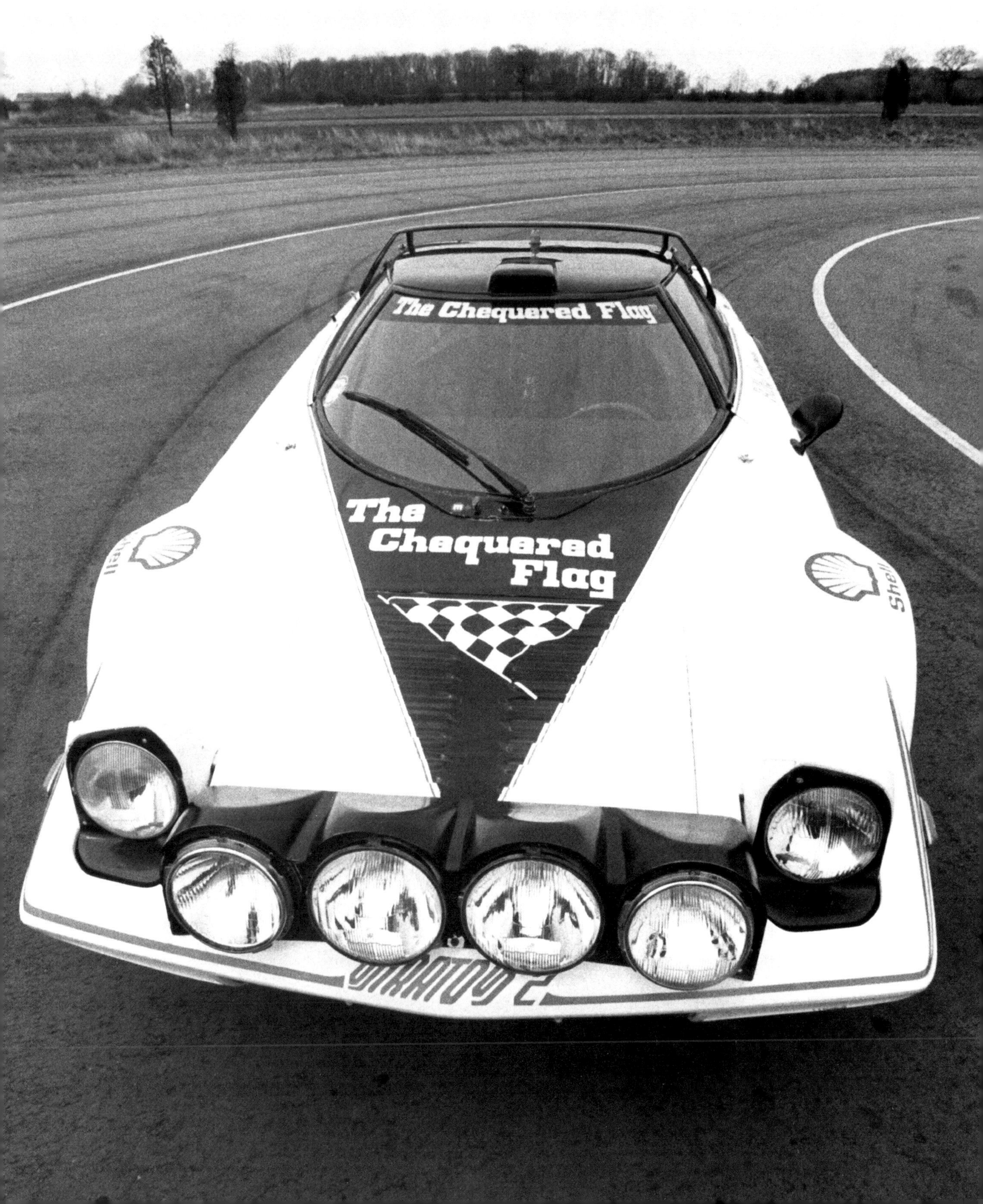
The Chequered Flag
The Chequered Flag
Shell
Shell

XI. Stealing the stage

Conventional wisdom has it that the magic ingredient to success is an unreasonably bloody-minded determination to keep going come hell or high water – and few team owners were ever as determined as Graham Warner. Chasing glory, however, came at a price. "I would estimate that by the end of 1976 I had already spent around £120,000 rallying the Lancias. And that is a conservative estimate."

Nevertheless, hopes were high going into 1977 and at least the season kicked off with a finish, as Billy Coleman and Peter Bryant came home eighth on

Billy Coleman and David Richards finished a lowly 15th on the 1977 Mintex Rally, but better results were just around the corner.

January's ShellSport Dean Rally. It was a heroic result, given that three stages had to be completed with a broken front upright.

Just as night follows day, the theme was set for the rest of the year, with the Stratos proving a frontrunner – but only so long as it held together. A month later, Coleman was teamed with co-driver Frank O'Donoghue as he attempted to win successive Galway International rallies. The 1977 running counted as a round of the European Rally Championship and attracted a quality field, although many entrants fell afoul of changing conditions. The low-slung Stratos was particularly ill-suited to the wet and narrow opening stages, often aquaplaning as grip was at a premium. More time was lost on the first day when an engine mounting broke. A quick fix was achieved, only for a bent gearbox shaft to hobble the car's performance the following day; Coleman had to complete five stages using only third gear. Nonetheless, at the end of the third and final day the Stratos had moved up the order to fourth overall. Unfortunately, he and wingman David Richards wouldn't be so fortunate later that same month, finishing an embattled fifteenth on the Mintex International Rally.

Coleman in particular hoped for better on his next event, April's Circuit of Ireland. However, his bid to claim a third win on this gruelling event was foiled by a bout of flu in the run-up to the start. Not only that, the organisers' prayers for a dry Easter went unanswered as Biblical levels of rain descended for much of the meeting. Not that Coleman appeared to notice, with only the perennial problem of a lack of available gears slowing him down. While Escort RS1800 duo Russell Brookes and John Brown would take a masterful win, Coleman and co-driver Peter Scott were fastest on 15 of the 54 stages to claim second place overall.

For the team's next event, May's Welsh Rally, Coleman and co-driver Richards would have a different mount. Warner recalls: "We were asked by Fiat to run the 131 on selected British rallies. The Stratos was getting all the headlines, which must have upset a few people with parent company Fiat. If it was going to pay the bills, Fiat wanted the glory! To my mind, we were recruited to act as an unofficial development team in the run up to that year's RAC Rally. We went through the whole car and made recommendations which ran to several pages, many of which were implemented. Not that we ever received any credit, you understand …"

Coleman spent five days at the Abarth competition department in Turin prior to the event, but was unable to test the car on gravel. Nonetheless, he put in some competitive times early on, despite the loss of fifth gear. The Fiat left the road on a repeat run of the Glynsaer stage during the final day. Ten minutes were lost extricating the car from a ditch and with it went the chance of a top five finish. Coleman and Richards

A Chequered Life

Previous page and right: Billy Coleman battled 'flu and variable conditions to finish second on the gruelling 1977 Circuit of Ireland aboard the 'Flag Stratos.

Coleman also had an occasional outing aboard a Fiat 131 Abarth in 1977. The car is seen here undergoing testing ahead of its May 1977 Welsh Rally debut.

would make amends a month later on the International Scottish Rally, claiming fourth place among 159 entrants despite an unusual problem. Pirelli had been on hand to offer assistance, with various combinations of tyre compounds being tested. "The issue wasn't with the rubber, it was the wheels," Warner recalls. "They kept breaking! Afterwards, we switched from the factory Campagnolo items to stronger Minilites which alleviated the problem."

June '77 saw a return trip to Ketterkenny for the three-day International Circuit of Donegal with Coleman and Austin Frazer emerging victorious in Stratos 2. They assumed the lead at half-distance and were never headed. Their advantage over eventual second place finishers Sean Campbell and Pat Speer was a remarkable two-and-a-half minutes. It was the 'Flag's second overall victory with a Lancia, the Stratos being brought out again for a run on the October's Castrol 77 event, only for a dropped inlet valve to bring Coleman's promising run to a premature halt.

Having taken a decisive World Rally Championship title over Ford, Fiat descended on the RAC Rally season finale armed with six 131s, with the 'Flag colours flying on those entered for three-time winner Timo Makinen, Timo Salonen, and Simo Lampinen. Warner recalls: "We demanded that since we had done a lot of work on the car, we should have our name on them. And despite what was written in the press at the time, we did have some of our boys working on the cars alongside the works mechanics. And just to make life really difficult for ourselves, we also ran Billy in the Stratos." Unfortunately, his promising early run was for nought thanks to a broken distributor, while Lampinen and co-driver Solve Andreason guided the first Fiat home in seventh place.

Heading into 1978, Warner enthusiasm was at a low ebb. "Running the Lancias was an expensive business and I was becoming disillusioned with all the breakages and so on. From a promotional point of view, the Stratos was great, but it was one large bill after another, hence the somewhat reduced calendar of events for that year."

Coleman was unstoppable on the 1977 International Circuit of Donegal, taking the lead at the halfway point and keeping Stratos 2 in front to the end of the three-day event.

Multiple-winner Timo Makinen drove a 131 in 'Flag colours on the 1977 RAC Rally, but failed to finish.

The season kicked off with fifth place on February's Galway International Rally for Coleman/O'Donoghue. A month later, Peter Scott returned to pace notes-reading duty for the Circuit of Ireland where they finished second overall to Escort RS1800 duo Russell Brookes/John Brown. A foray to Italy for the Rally 4 Regioni event in May ended in retirement for Coleman and one-time-only co-driver Renato Meiohas, Coleman re-teaming with Peter Scott to finish sixth in the 24 Hours of Ypres. There would be no further outings until October's TV-friendly Texaco Rallysprint event, in which Andy Dawson saw off a variety of contemporary rally and Formula One stars.

For '79, Warner hedged his bets and acquired an ex-John Haugland Triumph. "We were familiar with Triumph TRs so we bought one from the factory team in Abingdon. The Group 4 TR7 featured the 3.5-litre Rover V8 engine, and it really looked and sounded the part. It originally ran with a 16-valve 4-cylinder engine before being converted to the full V8-spec which is how we bought it. We then put the car in our colours."

Simo Lampinen's car was the sole survivor of the six factory-backed Fiat Abarths at the finish of the 1977 RAC Rally, placing seventh overall wearing 'Flag livery.

Right: Following a hefty crash on the 1978 International Circuit of Donegal, Stratos 2 was reconstructed by Don Fenwick into the unofficially-dubbed Stratos 3.

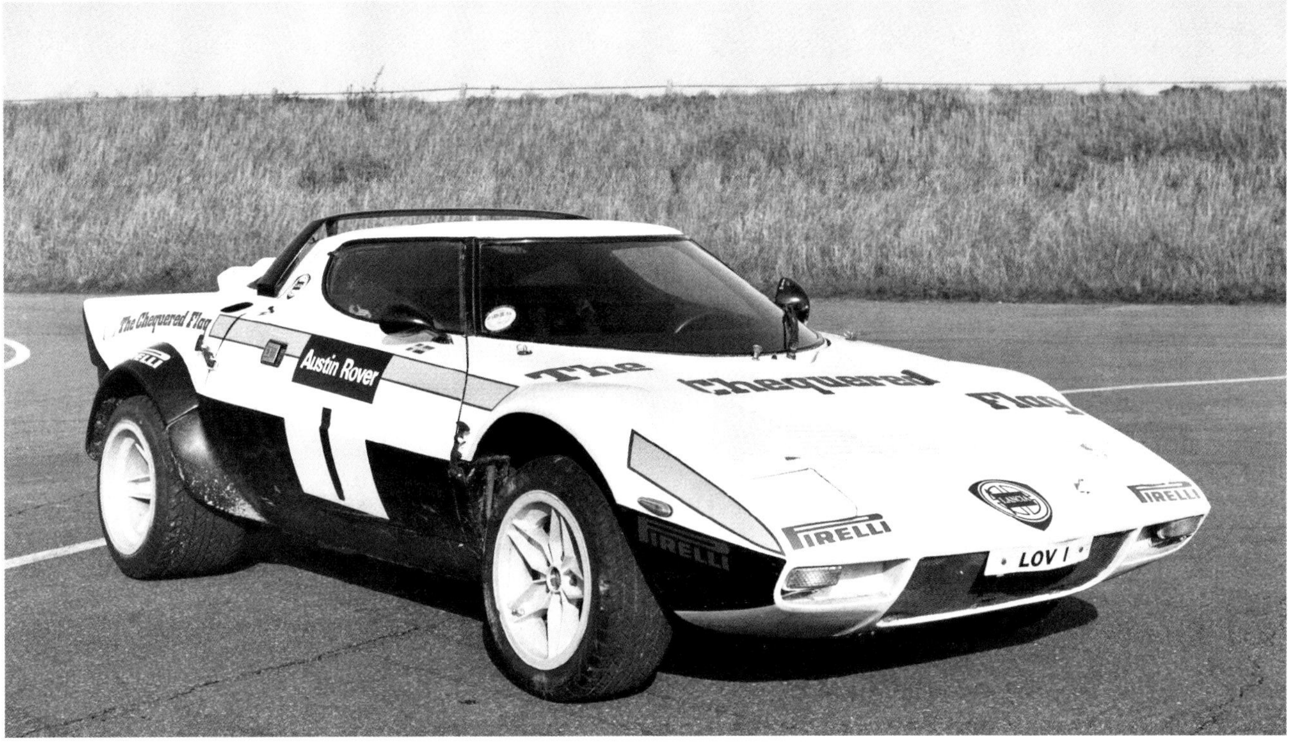
The Chequered Flag
Austin Rover
The Chequered Flag
PIRELLI
LOV 1

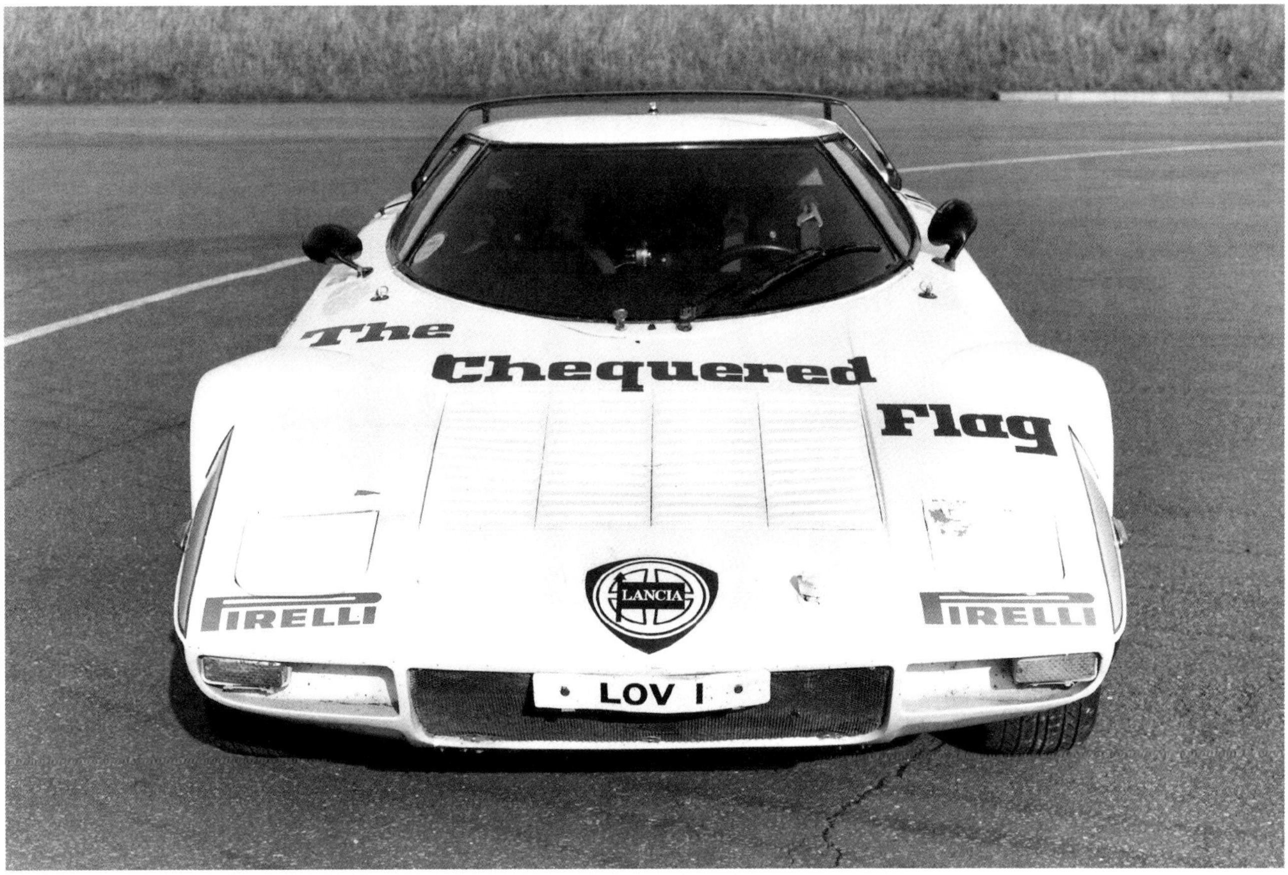
The Chequered Flag
LANCIA
PIRELLI
PIRELLI
LOV 1

The TR was entrusted to former Formula Ford champion Derek Boyd for the February 9-11 Galway International Rally, along with accomplished co-driver Fred Gallagher. Unfortunately, their rally was violently curtailed on the 14.7 mile Cleggan stage, barely two hours into the event. The Triumph connected with a stone wall, its occupants requiring hospitalisation. Boyd suffered broken ribs, Gallagher a broken pelvis. "It was an awful mess, and I'm only grateful that they survived," Warner recalls. "The car was straightened out and did the Circuit of Ireland that April, but it was sold on shortly thereafter. We also built a second car but by then I was beginning to lose interest."

It didn't help that Stratos 2 was all but destroyed in June's International Circuit of Donegal. The 'Flag chose to run the Lancia and the reconstructed Triumph, but almost didn't make the start thanks to a local petrol shortage and a postal strike which resulted in some competitors' entry forms going astray. A recuperated Boyd was installed in the TR7 V8, his run involving a fastest time on the Fanad Head stage between spins and expensive-sounding noises from under the bonnet. The Stratos would fare even worse. 'Flag old boy Cahal Curley came out of retirement to drive the Lancia, and must have wished he hadn't. On the first day, the car got out of shape along a particularly bumpy stretch of asphalt and veered into a ditch. It was back on the road inside a minute, but with a broken tie-rod. This was fixed at a service halt, but Curley then began to complain of a "... total absence of anchors," according to a *Motoring News* report. Even so, he manfully overcame this issue and appeared set to go the distance, only for disaster to strike with just four stages to go. The Stratos got out of shape on a fast-left bend, the nearside wheel striking a post which then flipped the car onto its back.

"It was a wreck," Warner recalls. "Fortunately for us, our seasoned and very talented engineer Don Fenwick had started to build up a road car around a damaged tub left over from an insurance rebuild. We took that and transferred all the best bits off our second car, although it carried the same chassis number. Don later built another Stratos based around a repaired tub for a customer. However, contrary to what I've read on the Internet, we never ran four rally Lancias."

Andy Dawson and Kevin Gormley debuted the reconfigured car on the 1980 Manx International Rally, finishing fourth. Still carrying the registration number OYU353R, but no longer bearing the legend Stratos 2 on its nose, the most striking feature was its right-hand drive set-up. "That was done for Billy Coleman who didn't like left-hand drive, but then he never drove it again so we converted it back to LHD. We did only a few more events, Rallysprints mostly, although Russell Brookes was fourth on the 1981 West Cork event. By that point it had our old reg number LOV1. Our final event was the 1982 Donington Rallyspint where it was driven by that year's Formula One World Champion Keke Rosberg and his Williams team-mate Derek Daly. The car was then sold to the Earl of Mexborough. And that was that, we were out of motorsport."

The 'Flag rounded out its competition programme with outings in the popular Rallysprints; legendary rally driver Björn Waldegård being among the many stars to drive a Stratos 3 on these knockout events.

But not out of the headlines, Warner having taken on a project that would change his life completely. "During the late '70s, I sponsored Robs Lamplough who was racing a BRM P25 Grand Prix car in historic events. I first met him back in the late '60s when we were running Formula Three cars and he was an enthusiastic privateer. One day in the spring of 1978, he casually mentioned that he 'had some Mustangs and Spitfires up at Duxford.' I admit I was a bit sceptical, but shortly thereafter I contacted the Imperial War Museum at Duxford. I was told that yes, they did know Mr Lamplough and yes, he did have various aircraft projects on site.

"In July of that year we flew to Silverstone aboard his Harvard to watch the British Grand Prix, the BRM having been entered in one of the support races. We had an enjoyable day, me catching up with old friends such as Frank Williams and Keith Duckworth, and Robs finishing third in his race. He then asked if I would be interested in accompanying him to Duxford to have a look at his various aircraft."

What he saw proved a real eye-opener. "If you didn't know any better, Robs' projects consisted of misshapen and rusty bits of metal fit only for scrap. We scrambled over heaps of damaged and corroded aluminium, along with assorted parts. They were the remains of three Israeli Spitfires which had crash-landed on the Golan Heights during the first Arab/Israeli war. They had been stripped of useful parts and then abandoned. Robs found the remains still lying there many years later, and the Israelis said, 'If you want to go to the trouble and expense of taking them away, then you are welcome to do so.' So he did just that! He also found a Russian T57 tank there, which he agreed to present to the IWM if they would settle the recovery costs, so he had all the aircraft etc shipped for free.

"In another hut were three P51 Mustang fuselages along with battered wings and tails, and assorted bits and pieces. We then walked into another hangar where Robs showed me his YAK 11, the Russian equivalent of the American T6 (Harvard) advanced fighter-trainer, which was undergoing a rebuild. Also being worked on was a Boeing B17 Fortress and a North American B25, but lurking in a corner was another derelict aircraft which was soon to assume a far greater importance and significance for me! There, laying on some old tyres, was the dusty main fuselage shell and gutted nose portion of a Bristol Blenheim, with some faded yellow paint and traces of an RAF roundel still just about visible. Stacked against the wall in the corner on more old tyres were two decrepit centre-sections, complete with rusty engine mountings and undercarriage frames. These triggered some distant memories from my days as an ATC cadet at school. I recognised the fuselage as belonging to a Blenheim due to the odd shape and asymmetrical framing of the nose where the glazing had once been.

"Haydon-Baillie had found both Blenheims in Canada in 1973. In fact, they had been built under license in Canada during the war. They had suffered greatly during the harsh winters, and had been either robbed of parts or vandalised, but he realised their importance and had the whole lot dismantled and shipped over to the UK in 1974. The Blenheim as an aircraft meant nothing to me, though. I could remember, albeit vaguely, reading that the RAF had used them as a stop-gap bomber at the beginning of the war, but I had never actually set eyes on one before."

Completely unbeknown to Warner at the time, this aircraft would come to dominate his life over the next 17 years.

"Later that morning, while in a hanger looking at the remains of Robs' Spitfires, I peered through the window into the workshop diagonally opposite. There sat the main fuselage and nose section of another Blenheim. It was clearly a sister to the one in the hanger, right down to its similarly faded yellow paint, although the fuselage was mounted on trestles and it had been partially stripped. Peering through the murky glass, I spied some rusty and dirty engines and a huge mound of other damaged airframe components. They all looked rather neglected, and then Rob informed me that what we had seen on our walkabout had been the basis for two long-term Blenheim projects, one a hoped-for restoration to possible flying condition, the other a proposed static exhibit. What's more, they had been abandoned as their owner, Ormond Haydon-Baillie, had been killed in an aircraft accident just over a year earlier. We then retired to the Chequers Inn at Fowlmere, where an idea began to take hold.

"I couldn't get those abandoned Blenheim remains out of my mind. I quizzed Robs about what was likely to happen to them, and about the set up at Duxford in general. Robs knew Ormond well, and told me that he had been a driving force behind several restoration projects at Duxford, so he would be sorely missed. He went on to explain that Ormond, like himself, had gathered a crew of keen volunteers to help with much of the maintenance work on the flying aircraft, and also on major restorations. It simply wasn't viable to have such work carried out at commercial rates. He then informed me that Ormond's family had, with great reluctance, decided to break up his collection of aircraft and aviation projects, as they wouldn't be able to continue with them. His brother Wensley would be acting for the estate in their dispersal and disposal.

"The situation was complicated further as the IWM was pressing for the removal of Ormond's aircraft and projects as it needed the space. This was proving difficult, as in those days aircraft preservation was still in its infancy. Finding a buyer for a larger collection of exotic machinery, much of which could be described as 'important restoration projects' was quite a task. On top of that, the family had begun talking of 'their occupancy rights as tenants,' and it began to get a bit tricky.

"It seemed to me an awful shame that the intended Blenheim restoration to flying condition had foundered, and I decided that I would at least

The Blenheim in Canada, ready for transportation to the UK after being acquired by Ormond Haydon-Baillie.

look into the possibility of taking it on myself. Robs became very excited when I mentioned this, telling me how wonderful the aircraft restoration scene was, and so on. His enthusiasm was infectious, and on the drive back to London I made up my mind that I would speak to Wensley Haydon-Baillie and the IWM so I had some idea of what I would be letting myself in for. My plan, if you could call it that, was to buy both aircraft and use the parts to make one airworthy. If sufficient parts were left over, there would also be a restored Blenheim for static display."

However, first he had to know what he was buying. "Wensley was receptive but as no inventory existed, he was a bit cagey when it came to the asking price. I hadn't been able to get near the second Blenheim, so after a few letters went backwards and forwards between the 'Flag and the IWM, I was allowed limited access to 'Blenheim Palace' to inspect the remains. It was all rather depressing. The main fuselage, which I had hitherto only seen though a dirty window, appeared structurally sound but had been stripped of its fittings. Various components lay around nearby: the tubular chassis for the pilot's seat and controls, along with the seat itself, the control column and rudder pedals. The rear fuselage section, complete with a bent tail fork wheel below and battered fin above, stood on the floor separated from the main fuselage, while a badly damaged wing, with most of the trailing-edge sections behind the rear spar missing altogether, rested on two trestles.

"We then went through a connecting passageway to view a mass of 20 engines and assorted components stored next door. This was even more discouraging – the engines were all as recovered and were caked in decades worth of oil, grease and dirt. There was also plenty of rust on steel components and white, crusty corrosion on the alloy parts. None of the engines were complete, missing items such as cylinder barrels, carburetors, manifolds, ignition harnesses, valve gear, magnetos; the list went on. Most had also lost the all-important engine-driven ancillary pumps for the oil, fuel, hydraulic, vacuum and pneumatic systems.

"The great pile of miscellaneous parts and bits and pieces from the airframes, engines and aircraft systems lay at the far end of the building. These comprised control rods and levers, yards of cables, pulleys, chains and sprockets; reams of electric wiring, switches and components, some broken instruments; numerous brackets and fittings, plus assorted lengths of pipework, hoses, oil- and fuel-lines and so on. These were all stripped from the nose and main fuselage sections, the engine and undercarriage bays etc, and had seemingly been discarded as being unfit for further use. Some of the other major airframe components situated around these mounds were more easily identifiable, but in an equally distressed and dilapidated condition. Main wheels and tyres with rusty brake drums, axles and brake shoes, two battered tail planes with the skeletal remnants of the elevator frames, plus two fins with part of the rudders having seemingly been gnawed at. There was also a section of the rear fuselage which included most of a turret and some dented fuel and oil tanks.

"Equally bent and battered were hundreds of pieces – both large and small – of aluminium in a wide variety of weird shapes and sizes; fragments of fairings, the partial cowlings, remnants of various skin panels and so on. It appeared to be a giant metallic jigsaw puzzle – one that was missing parts and lacked a picture to guide assembly!"

None of this dissuaded Warner, whose next step was to seek the advice of someone qualified to assess the probability – or even the possibility – of this pile of scrap metal ever taking to the skies again. "Firstly, I spoke with Norman Chapman, an ex-RAF fitter who had worked on many Blenheims during the war and was then rebuilding Robs' YAK 11. He was keen to see the Blenheim project rescued and pointed me towards his friend Fred Hanson, another ex-RAF fitter and fully licensed aircraft engineer. He had been responsible for signing off the Duxford-based B17 Flying Fortress 'Sally B,' among others. Fred would therefore be able to answer my one burning question – was the proposed restoration to airworthy status feasible or not?

"We arranged a meeting and Fred poked and prodded at the assorted bits and wrote ever-lengthening lists of what was missing and what needed to be done to return the Blenheim back to 'as new' condition. It became more and more depressing as Fred pointed out the main-wheel tyres were unserviceable and no longer made, the propellers were beyond repair and similarly unobtainable, and many other major items were either too badly damaged to repair or merely absent from this incomplete kit of parts. And of course there were no manufacturer's drawings, and no new replacement parts for either the engines or airframes were available. That much we had established during a brief preliminary survey, and it would only get worse.

"At the end of the day, we sat on a bench overlooking the peaceful, deserted airfield. Fred expressed major reservations, and explained that historic aircraft would have to be placed on the United Kingdom Civil Register so that the Civil Aviation Authority Surveyors could monitor and approve the work as it progressed. What's more, we would have to maintain detailed records so that they would be able – once entirely satisfied – to issue the Permit to Fly. However, as the words left his mouth I was already imagining the rebuilt Blenheim taking to the skies!"

The next step was for Warner to meet former members of Ormond's 'Black Knight' team of volunteers to see if they were willing to rejoin the project. It was back to the Chequers in Fowlmere. "John Romain, who would play such an important role in the years to come, stood out as much for his keenness as for the astute accuracy of his questioning. He was anxious to know if I had fully taken onboard the enormity of such an undertaking; would I become bored and walk away the moment the going got tough? I told John and the other guys that I was determined to complete the restoration. There was then the small matter of persuading the IWM to grant a lease on the workshop and to enter a rental agreement for part of the hangar space required for final assembly work. The IWM, however, wasn't interested. Following protracted negotiations, I was unable to obtain any form of lease or rental agreement from the Board of Trustees. As such, I had no security of tenure at all, which was worrying. I had to be content with an agreement, renewable on a three-year rolling basis, that they would make sufficient space available in return for our providing suitable aircraft – including the Blenheim during the course of the rebuild – on long-term loan to the IWM as public exhibits. I also negotiated further with Wensley, and agreed a mutually acceptable price for the remains. You could argue that I let my heart rule my head, and it would have been more sensible for me to simply walk away, but I couldn't. As the eternal optimist, I knew it would be worth whatever agonies came my way."

With agreements and contracts in place, Warner found himself the proud owner of two derelict Bristol

The Blenheim arrives in Duxford. The enormity of the project did not deter Warner and his crew.

Blenheims. The team also had a new identity, the boss coining the British Aerial Museum tag. "That soon became BAM, but with the sub-title of 'Flying Military Aircraft' to describe our main activity which, starting with the Blenheim, would in time be restoring and operating airworthy – as opposed to merely static – ex-military aircraft. We refitted Building 66 – invested in a kettle even! – and had the most wonderful crew. Aside from John Romain, who would in future years become managing director of our associated Aircraft Restoration Company, there was John Larcombe who was an ex-RAF pilot and someone with plenty of experience in everything from warbirds to Boeing 747 Jumbos. We appointed him our chief pilot in 1980. Then there was the ever-cheerful John 'Smudger' Smith who saw service with the RAF before doing research work for the Ministry of Aviation. He later joined the Hertfordshire Constabulary before returning to his first love. Smudge, who also happened to be a trained metalworker coachbuilder, straightened, repaired, rolled, wheeled and planished more panels, cowlings and fairings than I care to remember. His contribution would be immense. In fact, there were so many members of our team, it's hard to know where to start."

"Graham was a good guy to work for," Smith recalls, "and we all used to wonder what kind of exotic car he would turn up in. Right from the start, he was very enthusiastic, but restoring the Blenheim wasn't about him; it wasn't an ego thing. He was always self-effacing in that respect. It was a team effort and he would be quick to point that out. It also helped that he had – and indeed still has – a sense of humour. He was the guiding force behind getting the Blenheim back in the air. It wouldn't have happened without him.

"What you have to remember about historic aircraft is that you can't just create a replica and take to the skies. The Civil Aviation Authority won't let you. If you restore an aircraft, it has to be repaired exactly to original specification; no deviation. To help with this, we managed to get together the few repair and maintenance manuals we could find from the Fitton and Fairchild companies, as the original and licensee manufacturers, together with all the RAF and RCAF manuals, notes and diagrams on the airframes, engines, props, and so on. We began the restoration with the centre section – which is the largest single portion of the entire aircraft – that was in 1979. From there it was a case of simply plugging away. We all knew it wouldn't be easy, but we all wanted to see a Blenheim in the air again."

Unfortunately, Warner was about to suffer a grievous loss which threatened to scupper the Blenheim from ever flying again.

Stratos and the team's second Triumph TR7 V8 flank a Beech 18. Warner turned his full attention to the historic aircraft movement in the early 1980s.

XII. The reckoning

With the 'Flag's rally campaigns now consigned to history, the early '80s should have been a period of relative calm for Graham Arthur Warner. The Blenheim project was under way, and the core retail business had ditched the Lancia franchise in favour of Opel. Lancia's reputation had been tarnished by the rust scandal that took hold in the late '70s. "It was a ridiculous situation, whereby cars weren't rustproofed properly, if at all, and were often stored for months on end out in the open. I remember engine mounts dissolving and worse. I knew that once the daily scandal rags got a sniff on the story, it would be game over. And of course they had a field day. We couldn't go on with Lancia – it was hurting our reputation, too – so I started looking around. I was taken with the Opel Manta and Monza coupés, and reasoned that the General Motors parent company would be a safe bet."

It was anything but. Sales were buoyant, the profit margin rather less so, and worse was to come. "At the end of 1984, the Chequered Flag became the subject of an unwelcome and enforced takeover. That came about as we had put our General Motors franchise on the market, with the firm's consent. Much to my annoyance, we had been pressured into selling Vauxhalls alongside Opels, which didn't sit well with me. I'd wanted to sell Opels because there were sporting models in the range. I had no interest in the Vauxhall sister brand. As far as I was concerned, Vauxhalls were the white goods of the car world. Although we sold hundreds of cars each year, GM's system of target-related bonuses – whereby they raised the target each time we reached it – and without which the dealership could not operate profitably, made the franchise a barely viable treadmill. We had superb sales and servicing facilities operating from separate showrooms and specially-built workshop premises near Chiswick Park Station, but the new car dealership had not, regrettably, been formed into a separate limited company. A potential buyer for the GM part of our business enquired about additionally purchasing the sports car core business, which had its own dedicated showrooms and workshops. I said, 'Sorry, it isn't for sale.'

"However, the finance company, whose stocking plan we were obliged to use to carry the high levels of stock required, suddenly demanded instant repayment. The small print of the agreement revealed that it was entitled to do so. As we were unable to pay off the large sum concerned, they appointed a receiver/manager to find a buyer for the company. As such, the entire 'Flag enterprise, including the main sports car business which I had no desire to sell and

The reckoning

which was operating at a profit, was sold over our heads. It was acquired by the same company that had been interested in the GM dealership and which had also wanted to buy the sports car business.

"I was extremely unhappy at this situation, to put it mildly. I felt that collusion had occurred, the net result being that I was left out in the cold, having lost the capital I had invested in the company. I stayed on for a short period as general manager for the new owners, but I felt as though I had lost my sense of identity, so I left to dabble in the classic car world. Having my life's work taken from me was incredibly upsetting, and selling cars from home didn't hold my interest for long. But as one door was closing, another opened to a more satisfying future."

Indeed, there was always aircraft. "The Blenheim project by then stood in the company's books at around £250,000; the new owners were not at all interested, and instructed that the partially completed project be sold. As I was unable to raise the book figure required, the accountants put it out to public tender, seeking far more than the sum I had been able to offer. This action further prolonged the uncertainty over the project's future, and unsettled the team even more. Five months then went by before the twice extended closing date for the tender was reached in April 1985. The accountants claimed to have received 'strong interest from overseas,' and the thought of our beloved Blenheim – into which we had all put so much that we regarded it as 'ours' – leaving for foreign parts was extremely upsetting.

"Fortunately, the other aircraft operated by BAM were owned by me and not the 'Flag, so were unaffected by this uncertainty. It was an awful time for all of us, and following a degree of arm-twisting I put in a higher bid which I could only afford by cashing-in life insurance policies. You can only imagine how relieved I was when my last-minute tender proved successful. That was followed almost immediately by the realisation that I now had to finance the vast amount of work still required from my own pocket directly, rather than indirectly as before."

As such, Warner and his team began seeking more effective ways of containing the costs. "We badgered suppliers so that we could buy our materials selectively and do all the work ourselves, rather than placing some items with outside contractors. We did this successfully. For instance, we had been quoted a large sum for repairing the oil tanks, and an even greater figure for the main fuel tanks, so we did them ourselves. We purged them thoroughly, removed all dents and welded up any splits in the alloy, renewed the filler-cap gaskets, pressure-tested them, and finally repainted them – the oil tanks yellow and the fuel-tanks green. The metalworking and alloy-welding expertise of Smudger Smith was pivotal to these processes. I'm proud of the fact that with one major exception, the entire Blenheim restoration was carried out by the team in-house."

The team also set about courting commercial sponsorship, and achieved one notable success. "John Romain and John Larcombe persuaded the Propeller Division of BAe [British Aerospace] at Lostock to rebuild the Blenheim's propellers as a training exercise," Warner recalls. "The cost of such work would otherwise have been prohibitive. The rebuilt and

The aircraft's centre section is seen here being stripped ready for inspection and repair.

A wing is seen being stripped of paint and readied for repair. Corrosion on the wing spars was a major headache for the team.

certified props looked brand new, the workmanship second to none. Lostock had previously been a factory operated by de Havilland (Propellers) Ltd, and we were able to establish from the stamped numbers that the props had been manufactured there in 1940 before being shipped by wartime convoy to Canada.

"John Romain had by now become a self-employed aircraft engineer, and did work for other warbird owners at Duxford. He charged BAM only for the hours he spent on the Blenheim, although he still spent most of his time on it. Meanwhile, I found a partner who purchased a half share in a Westland Lysander and we took on outside work to help offset the overheads. We gradually became involved in film and photographic work, as well as participating in air displays. All income generated from these endeavours went straight into the Blenheim."

Aside from the constant struggle to attract financial support, one critical problem arose concerning the actual

rebuild. "At more than one stage, it looked as though we would be unable to repair the steel portions of the main wing spars. Each outer wing had two full-depth one-piece spars which bolted onto the straight centre-section spars at the engine/undercarriage mounting frames, and extended to the wing tips, tapering accordingly. The main vertical webs were made of a heavy alloy with light alloy stiffeners, and these webs presented no problem. However, they were supported structurally by load-bearing angle spar-booms, which formed a 'T' shape to the top and bottom of each web. These were made from a special high-tensile spring steel, parts of which had suffered from years of exposure to the elements. One or two areas of surface corrosion were apparent, and stripping them down revealed far more serious areas of internal corrosion.

"This raised the question of where to obtain some of this special steel. Discussions with experts and stockists convinced us that not only was none available, but also that no modern equivalent was being made anywhere to this obsolete specification. We were therefore overjoyed when, following extensive enquiries at BAe, someone managed to locate a few short lengths of this original steel for us. However, the CAA insisted that we could only repair the small affected area on the 20ft boom or cornice sections by means of a one-piece replacement of the entire section, and then only with steel exactly to the manufacturer's specification. Despite our pleas, the much shorter lengths that we now had, which were ready to be shaped and fitted, were deemed unacceptable.

"This did seem like the end of the road, but John's persistence and ingenuity paid off when a Good Samaritan at BAe discovered an old wartime Bristol Aeroplane Company 'Battle Damage Repair Manual'. It illustrated with a series of line drawings exactly the type of localised splicing repair to the booms and cornices that were required, and gave details of the official methods to affect them, showing that we could carry them out at the joints between the lengths of material that were at our disposal. The CAA accepted this repair scheme as it had been issued by the original 'Design Authority', and we were allowed to proceed in accordance with it. Phew!"

However, the BAM team wasn't out of the woods just yet. "Due to the curvature of the wing profile, none of 'T' shaped steel booms were at right angles to the webs. In fact, all eight had different angles, and as such had to be rolled exactly to these differing profiles, as did the supporting cornices, no two of which were alike. The shaped steel had to be heat-treated and hardened, which is where we hit another brick wall. We had these new sections already annealed, cut and shaped to the complex profiles as required, but only one company in the UK had an oven large enough to accept our 6ft sections for the heat treatment. These carefully shaped sections had to be heated up to 860 degrees Celsius and oil-quenched, then air-quenched to 460 degrees Celsius. Unfortunately for us, the sections distorted during the cooling down process, which rendered them useless. We had just enough left to carry out the approved repair to the starboard wing, which accounted for the last of limited supply of original steel."

It was back to square one. "We did the rounds of searching for stockists. I was referred to Rheinmetall, near Essen, Germany. I called them and was shunted between departments until a man came on who knew what I was talking about. I quoted the lengthy specification number, he looked it up on their records and came back with, 'Ah yes, zis steel was used in ze Blenheim, ze Beaufort and ze Beaufighter!' To my delight, they confirmed that they would be able to manufacture some for us to that spec."

There was, however, a condition – the minimum order had to be for 30 tonnes. "That clearly wasn't going to happen but, upon hearing this – and to his great credit – the chairman of the British Steel Corporation then arranged for a small batch to be made at one of his mills in 6ft lengths.

"Even when the spars had been rebuilt, we still had to rebuild and re-skin the rest of wings and perform countless other tasks. At each juncture we appeared to hit a seemingly insurmountable obstacle, only to come good after much perseverance. The primary reason for this was the hard work of John Romain and Smudger Smith, plus Colin Swan who was responsible for the electrical and hydraulic systems, and engine man Neville Gardner. Without their dogged determination, the Blenheim would have remained grounded forever."

The dedication shown by the largely voluntary team of restorers was tested on an almost daily basis. What is written here is just a thumbnail sketch of what was involved. The story behind how they sourced everything from tyres (which had long since become obsolete), to the saga behind getting two functional Bristol Mercury radial engines and their geared superchargers to operational condition are covered in depth in Warner's 1996 book, *Spirit of Britain First*.

Then came the big day, which for the boss at least was freighted with anxiety. "John Larcombe took a short leave from his job as Training Captain with British Airways. The usually cheerful John Romain looked increasingly fretful, feeling the weight of responsibility as he racked his brain to see if he had overlooked anything. Both Johns were ready to go, but then the British weather let us down."

May '87 had been particularly damp and dull, but late in the afternoon of May 22, a window appeared in the otherwise inclement weather. "It was just wide enough for us to allow the first flight. The two Johns strapped themselves into the cockpit, taxied

A repaired wing nearing completion. Sourcing the correct materials – and at a price that wasn't prohibitive – would prove a test of initiative for Warner and his team.

A mighty 9-cylinder radial engine at the final assembly stage.

Getting a new wiring loom manufactured and fitted was just one of the many hurdles the team at Duxford had to clear.

Nearing completion: this atmospheric late night shot shows the Blenheim only months away from its maiden post-restoration flight.

The Blenheim's engines are tested for the first time – successfully so.

out, carried out engine tests and their pre-take off cockpit drill. All pressures and temperatures were good; all systems go. They lined up at the threshold of the runway, received permission from the control tower to take off, and then John Larcombe opened the throttles smoothly and the Blenheim accelerated down the runway. The engine note rose, the tail came up, and we all held our breath as the magical moment for which we had been waiting for so long had arrived. And then, just as she was about to become airborne, John throttled back and abandoned the take-off. It was nothing serious: the under-nose escape hatch hadn't been secured properly.

"They then taxied back to the other end of the runway and tried again. John opened the throttle, the Blenheim accelerated, the engine note rose, the tail came up, and this time it lifted cleanly. She was airborne! We all cheered, slapped each other on the back and then cheered some more. We had done it! She flew beautifully. John returned to Duxford and did a few fly-pasts and low passes to our great delight. Then, with wheels and flaps down, he performed a beautiful three-point landing. John taxied back to a rapturous welcome and opened the champagne which had been carried on that first flight. We drank from plastic cups and ignored the rain that was falling once again."

This would, however, be a triumph stripped of euphoria. With exhaustive flight tests procedures completed, and having been granted a Permit to Fly, the Blenheim participated in its first-ever public display to great acclaim at the Biggin Hill Air Fair on June 6-7 1987. A week later, the aircraft was due to appear at both the Duxford Military Display and at the Guild of Air Pilots and Air Navigators event at North Wield. "We had more than a dozen other confirmed air display bookings for the rest of year including the big International Air Tattoo at Fairford," Warner recalls. "We also had strong interest from organisers for the following year. The income generated by these events would start to repay BAM for the enormous expenditure sunk into the Blenheim, and I informed our bank manager that we would soon be able to reduce our rather bloated overdraft."

Then disaster stuck. Chief pilot Lancombe was unable to attend the Duxford and North Wield events due to a scheduling conflict with British Airways, so reserve pilot Roy Pullan took his place at the controls. "My choice of pilot was somewhat restricted by the insurance company," Warner says. "I would have loved to have flown the Blenheim myself, but I was deemed to be insufficiently experienced. Roy was a 'dyed-in-the-wool' aircraft enthusiast who had been involved with the Blenheim restoration over a four or five year

period, fabricating the bomb doors in his shed, and preparing the moulds for the cockpit glazing. More importantly, he was a vastly experienced pilot who had just retired as a British Airways Senior Captain. He was also familiar with all manner of tailwheel piston aircraft, and as such he was welcomed by our insurers."

On June 21 1987, Warner and the BAM team's world would be turned upside down. "I was waiting at Duxford with keen anticipation for the Blenheim to return from the display at Denham and perform the first public display at Duxford. It had been arranged with the organisers of both events that Roy would fly straight into his planned display slot at the Duxford Military Show, and the timings of both shows were carefully co-ordinated to accommodate this. We then scanned the skies at the appointed time, but an announcement over the PA then beckoned me over to the control tower. I was greeted with the shocking news that the Blenheim had crashed badly and that the crew members were in hospital. My concern was for the crew, all of whom were good friends. I was therefore relieved to hear that their injuries weren't critical. I raced down to Hillingdon Hospital to see John Romain and Smudger Smith, and then on to High Wycombe to see Roy, but he had been sedated.

"Smudger told me that Roy had been attempting a 'touch and go' landing, whereby a landing is followed by an immediate take off – or 'go around again' – without allowing the aircraft to roll to a rest. This isn't a suitable manoeuvre to be performed at air displays, and this was the fundamental cause of the accident: the Blenheim had hit a tree and cartwheeled across Denham Golf Course. Fortunately, it hadn't caught fire, but her back was broken, the nose was completely smashed, and both engines had been torn away. I went down to the golf course and she just sat there, twisted and scarred, with pieces of wreckage strewn a hundred yards behind her. Members of the BAM team were also there. They were simply devastated, a bit tearful, and in a state of shock."

Inevitably, this trauma was exacerbated by the insurance company looking to wriggle out of its responsibilities. If that wasn't enough, the Accident Investigation Branch of Department of Transport, plus the Legal of Airworthiness Departments of the Civil Aviation Authority began scrutinising all aspects of the team's operation of the aircraft to establish the precise cause of the crash with a view to instigating prosecutions. In time, blame would be apportioned to Pullan, who was charged with contravening Articles 47 and 48 or the Air Navigation Oder whereby, "A person shall not recklessly or negligently cause an aircraft to endanger any person or property," or, "… recklessly or negligently endanger an aircraft and the persons therein." He was tried and convicted of these criminal offences, fined heavily, and ordered to pay substantial prosecution costs, but that did not help BAM.

"It's hard to discuss Roy impartially as he was a charming family man and we enjoyed socialising together," Warner says. "I was aware that he suffered the occasional rush of blood to the head so I take responsibility for putting him in the Blenheim. He committed several serious lapses of good airmanship, made grave errors of judgment, mishandled the engines, and then failed to retain any control whatsoever, so it was a case of pure human error. He let his ego get in the way; it was a needless accident that should never have happened."

There was now the small matter of whether to restore the Blenheim once again, or to simply walk away. For Warner and the BAM team, the latter option was inconceivable. Having agreed terms to buy the 'write-off' from the insurance company, an airframe and outer wings were sourced, but there was still a mountain to climb. In order to help alleviate the financial burden, The Blenheim Society was formed in June 1988. The organisation held its first public meeting five months later and 350 people – including many ex-Blenheim crews – descended on the Officers' Mess at Duxford to show their support.

Nonetheless, money remained tight and the enormity of what lay ahead served to test the BAM squad's staying power. "We made a rod for our own backs by setting ourselves the target of completing the second restoration in only five years," Warner says. "Strictly speaking, I made the rod by talking publically about the timeframe! John Romain then drew up the rebuild programme and work schedules. As the CAA-licensed engineer responsible, he supervised all of the actual work by the volunteers – he did the lion's share of the work himself – and rose to the occasion magnificently. We were all very much aware that the CAA would be keeping a beady eye on the project in light of what had happened."

To dismiss the second restoration in just a few paragraphs would be to do the team a disservice, but the subject is well covered in Warner's *Spirit of Britain*

Left: Taking to the skies! The Blenheim returned to its natural habitat in May 1987, only to crash back down to earth shortly thereafter.

A Chequered Life

First. "Essentially, it was a re-run of the first restoration," he recalls. "We had the benefit of experience and familiarity with the aircraft, but there would be no short cuts. It was a real struggle all the way, but in 1993 we were ready to take to the skies again."

However, there had been some sadness along the way, not least the loss of John Larcombe, who died in June 1990 after crashing a P63 King Cobra on his return from a French air show. "He showed remarkable bravery and skill after the engine failed," Warner recalls. "He managed to miss a residential area, but sadly lost his life in the ensuing accident."

With the restoration complete, there was one last 'T' to cross. "We had decided that the initial markings would be coded 'WM-Z', after the 'personal' Blenheim Mk IV-F of Wing Commander The Hon 'Max' Aitken DFC, the son of the wartime Minister of Aircraft Production, and proprietor of *The Daily Express*, Lord Beaverbrook. They were used when he was CO of 68 Squadron. I wrote to his widow, Lady Violet Aitkin, to obtain her consent and she gladly gave her blessing."

And so, on Friday, May 28 1993, with myriad tests performed, it was time for the big reveal. Some 5000 people descended on Duxford to witness the only airworthy Blenheim return to the skies. Lord Rothermere was also on hand to say a few well-chosen words in memory of his grandfather and to praise the BAM team, before Lady Aitken opened the champers and poured some over the aircraft's nose. What the public didn't know was that the team only received the Permit to Fly less than an hour before the allotted take off time! Romain, joined by Nev Gardner, then put on a smooth but spirited display, which was greatly appreciated by the 500-strong ex-Blenheim crews in attendance.

"It was a fantastic day and one which I think moved quite a few people. Restoring the Blenheim had been a huge undertaking the first time, but to do it twice speaks volumes about the men who gave up so much of their time to make it airworthy. Over the next few years we participated in countless air displays and, sadly, a great many closing ceremonies of famous RAF stations such as Wattisham, West Raynham and Swanton Morley. In 1995 the Blenheim performed in the VE Day celebrations at Duxford, Southend and Chatham, and in the televised fly-past over Buckingham Palace. I was in the bomb-aimer's position in the nose and remember quite clearly seeing HM the Queen, the Queen Motor and the Princess Royal on the balcony."

In October of that year, the UK enjoyed something of an Indian summer. The Autumn Air Show at Duxford witnessed a huge crowd enjoying unseasonably glorious weather. The Blenheim, flanked closely by a Hurricane and a Spitfire, led a formation fly-past as a memorial to those who lost their lives in the Battle of Britain. The trio flew in from the west, low and tight, against a canvas of cloud-freckled blue sky, the

ageless vistas of the Duxford countryside unfolding behind them. Merlin and Mercury engines on open exhausts scored the scene, a splendid spectacle that brought to life the history of Great Britain's finest hour back in 1940. Everyone there was moved by the experience, the commentator adding: "These three aircraft form the perfect flying tribute to all of the RAF pilots and aircrews who served during the war."

For Warner, that was all that mattered: "We had honoured those brave souls who did so much to protect us from tyranny. Unquestionably, it had been worth the emotional rollercoaster, and more."

Showing remarkable fortitude, Warner and the BAM team restored the Blenheim a second time. It is seen here in the colours of the 'personal' Blenheim flown during wartime by Wing Commander The Hon 'Max' Aitken DFC.

The Queen Mother meets the BAM team, congratulating them on their achievement in restoring the Blenheim.

The Blenheim was used extensively for air displays during the 1990s, appearing at several closing ceremonies such as RAF Swanton Morley in 1994. From left-right: Pilot 'Hoof' Proudfoot, seen here with Air Marshal Sir John Allison and Warner.

Postscript

Anyone who knows Graham Warner will tell you that he is ambivalent about celebrity. He never was a fame-chasing self-publicist, instead preferring to let motorsport promote his business rather than the team principal. However, following the loss of the 'Flag and the move into the historic aircraft arena, he became detached from the world of race tracks and special stages. Indeed, he freely admits that for a long time he deliberately distanced himself from motorsport, and batted away offers from authors keen to tell his story. For a man blessed with such a deep understanding of motorsport history, he had little understanding of his place in it. Aside from being an accomplished driver, he was a facilitator to whom so many drivers, co-drivers, mechanics and administrators owe a huge debt. It just took a long time for him to recognise the esteem in which he is held, and why enthusiasts might want to read about him.

It was only after his retirement in the early '90s that Graham began to reappear within the motorsport community, occasionally giving interviews to the specialist press – not just to British publications – and well-received presentations to car clubs. But even then, he had no desire to produce a book outlining his career. The truth is, he was more than capable of writing it himself. Indeed, despite his notional retirement, he soon became an in-demand journalist and author, writing about aircraft and aviation history for publications such as *FlyPast* and *Classic Aircraft*. His first book, *The Forgotten Bomber: Story of the Restoration of the World's Only Airworthy Bristol Blenheim,* was published in 1991, his second effort *Spirit of Britain First: The Dramatic 20 Year Quest to Return a Bristol Blenheim to the Skies* arriving five years later. He then followed that with the nine years in the making *The Bristol Blenheim A Complete History* which, following its critically-acclaimed reception in 2002, was revised and enlarged for the second edition.

Around that time, Graham and wife Shirley downsized from their home in Ashdon near Saffron Waldon to a new house in Storrington on the South Downs in West Sussex, which is where the author first met them in 2004. Both were very welcoming to a *Motor Sport* features editor with a keen interest in the many cars that Graham raced or fielded. It was therefore an honour to be asked to write this book the better part of a decade later. Sadly, within weeks of us embarking on this project in January 2011, Shirley passed away following a long battle with osteoarthritis, which, for obvious reasons, meant the book was temporarily put on hold. Graham and Shirley had been married for 58 years, but with typical stoicism, he regrouped and insisted we resume operations. We did just that, despite a further move to an apartment in Sunningdale, Berkshire and a debilitating stroke in early 2012, which Graham was fortunate to survive. With equal predictability, he had regained his speech within a few months and was determined to get back up to speed with the latest gossip from the pit lane.

What is clear is that Graham Arthur Warner has packed in enough action, drama and intrigue over the years to last several lifetimes.

Also from Veloce Publishing ...

Inspired to Design

F1 cars, Indycars & racing tyres: the autobiography of **Nigel Bennett**

Foreword by Rick Mears. Contributions from Bruce Ashmore, Nigel Beresford and Chuck Sprague

Nigel Bennett's unique autobiography describes his life and career, from growing up influenced by car design, to his education and the building of his 750 specials. He describes his work as Firestone Development Manager, recounting many tales of the outstanding designers and drivers of the period. Detailing his work in Formula 1, as a Team Lotus engineer, and then as Team Ensign designer, he also covers his Indycar designs at Theodore, Lola Cars and Penske Cars. Life after his retirement, his involvement in boat design and with modern F1 teams, are also recounted.

ISBN: 978-1-845845-36-0 • Hardback • 25x20.7cm
£35* UK/$54.95* USA • 176 pages • 194 colour and b&w pictures

For more info on Veloce titles, visit our website at www.veloce.co.uk
email: info@veloce.co.uk • Tel: +44(0)1305 260068
* prices subject to change, p&p extra

Also from Veloce Publishing ...

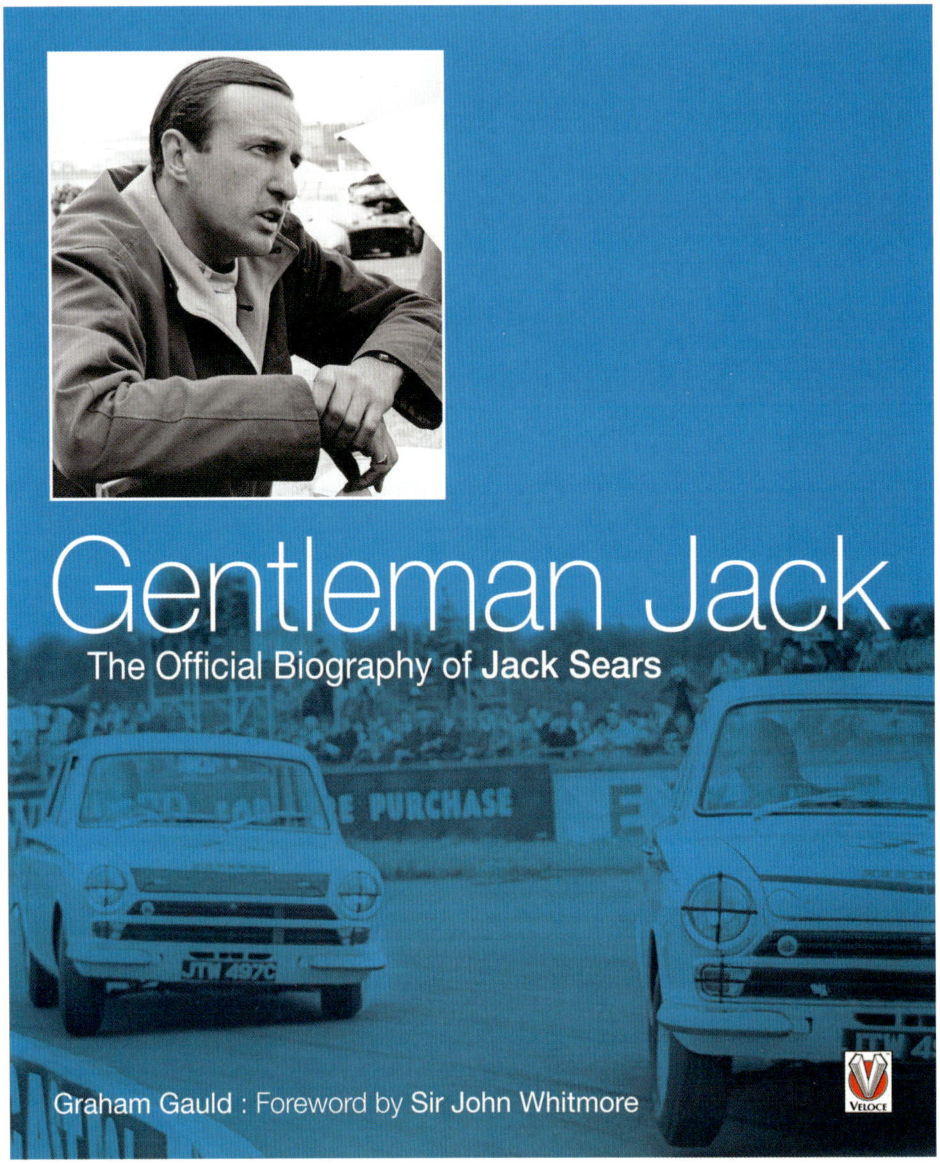

Gentleman Jack
The Official Biography of Jack Sears
Graham Gauld : Foreword by Sir John Whitmore

Gentleman, entrepreneur, and excellent racing driver, here is the fascinating story of John 'Jack' Sears, or Gentleman Jack as he was popularly known. Packed with facts direct from the man himself, and illustrated with 150 unique photos, this is a must-have piece of motoring history.

ISBN: 978-1-84584-151-5
Hardback • 25x20.7cm • £24.99* UK/$49.95* USA • 160 pages
• 154 colour and b&w pictures

For more info on Veloce titles, visit our website at www.veloce.co.uk
email: info@veloce.co.uk • Tel: +44(0)1305 260068
* prices subject to change, p&p extra

Also from Veloce Publishing ...

A unique collection of behind-the-scenes stories and anecdotes as told, in their own words, by former Grand Prix mechanics who have worked at the top level of the sport during the past 50 years.
On the front line of the sport, mixing with drivers and team bosses, they saw a side of it that nobody else got to see and rarely gets to hear about – and this book tells their story, supplemented by photographs from the archives and photo albums of the mechanics themselves, many of which are previously unpublished.

ISBN: 978-1-84584-199-7
• Paperback • 21x14.8cm • £12.99* UK/$24.95* USA • 176 pages • 89 colour and b&w pictures

For more info on Veloce titles, visit our website at www.veloce.co.uk
email: info@veloce.co.uk • Tel: +44(0)1305 260068
* prices subject to change, p&p extra

Also from Veloce Publishing ...

Return to Glory!
The Mercedes-Benz 300 SL Racing Car

Robert Ackerson

The 300 SL's 1952 debut was the culmination of a long, difficult road back to racing for Mercedes-Benz after a 13 year break. This book vividly depicts the 300 SL's performance in the five races in which it competed in that year, and tells the story of how it became the most successful competition sports car that season. Through dramatic photographs and stirring text, one of the greatest years of sports car racing is brought to life, filled with automobiles prepared by great factory teams, driven by men who were national sporting idols, and raced under gruelling conditions unique to the age.

ISBN: 978-1-845846-17-6
Hardback • 25x25cm • £75* UK/$120* USA • 144 pages • 126 colour and b&w pictures

For more info on Veloce titles, visit our website at www.veloce.co.uk
email: info@veloce.co.uk • Tel: +44(0)1305 260068
*prices subject to change, p&p extra

Index

AC Cobra
  (289) 86-89, 91, 94
  (427) 94, 95, 97, 99, 106
Adams, Len 38
Anstead, John 27
Arundell, Peter 43, 49-52, 58, 60, 73, 77, 79, 82
Ashdown, Peter 51, 54, 61
Ashley, Ian 108-110, 113, 114, 116, 118, 119
Aston Martin
  2-litre Speed Model 21, 22
  DB4GT Zagato 66, 73-75
Austin-Healey 100S 27-30
Autosport World Cup 33, 38, 39, 47-50, 62

Baghetti, Giancarlo 59
Baillie, Sir Gawaine 32
Baird, Gil 34
Beattie, Chas 41, 103, 124
Beckwith, Mike 65, 83, 97, 99, 103, 106
Beuttler, Mike 28, 34, 45-48, 50, 51, 54, 56
Bloxham, Jean 28
Bloxham, Roy 34
Bolster, John 77
Bondurant, Bob 87, 89, 93, 95, 96, 103
Bowmeester, Ad 62
Boyd, Derek 136
Brabham, Jack 82
Bridger, Tommy 47, 48
Briggs, David 27
Brighton Speed Trials 30
Bristol Blenheim 137-141, 143-145, 148-150
British Aerial Museum (BAM) 140, 143, 144, 148, 149
Broadley, Eric 51, 66
Brown, John 38
Bugatti Type 59 11, 12

Chapman, Colin 32, 40, 41, 59, 66, 75, 76, 79, 111
Chequered Flag, The
  Business 24-26, 32, 38, 52, 53, 74, 80, 130, 142, 143
  Chequered Flag-McLaren Racing Team 108
  Engineering 38
  Stable 27, 28, 31, 42
Clark, Jim 33, 34, 38-41, 45, 49, 51, 73, 76, 79, 82, 89, 111
Clarke, Rodney 4, 12
Cliff Davis Cars 38, 45
Coleman, Billy 130, 131, 133, 134, 136
Connaught (marque) 11, 20
Cooper Monaco 31, 32, 42
Costin, Frank 74
Costin, Mike 29, 32, 39
Cosworth
  DFV 41
  Engineering 32, 39, 41, 59
Courage, Piers 86, 88, 90, 96, 99, 103
Crabb, Percy 27-31, 42
Curley, Cahal 120, 121, 125, 127

DAF F3 car 101, 103, 106
Dale, Jim 103
Daly, Derek 126
Dawson, Andy 124, 134, 136
De Adamich, Andrea 103
Dickson, Tommy 45, 48, 49
Duckworth, Keith 32, 39, 40, 61, 76, 136
Duke, Geoff 45, 46, 48, 50, 54

Entebbe Raid 127
Enthwhistle, Tommy 62
Epps, Harry 43
European Cup Challenge 83

Fairman, Jack 27
Fangio, Juan Manuel 96
Fangio, Oscar 'Cacho' 96
Fenwick, Don 136
Fergusson, Pat 34, 38, 48, 62
Fiat 131 Abarth 131, 133
Foster, Alan 27, 29, 34, 38, 42, 47
Fry-Climax 52

Gardner, Frank 62, 65, 112, 113
Gaston, Paddy 47
Gemini
  Gemini-BMW 34
  Mk2 35- 39, 41-43, 45, 48, 50
  Mk3/3A 48, 53, 54, 57, 60, 61, 65, 67, 68
  Mk4 66, 67, 72, 73, 77
Gethin, Peter 89, 91, 92, 106
Gibson, Dick 43, 64
Granger, Bill 92
Grant, Gregor 33, 58, 82, 86, 97
Greene, Keith 61

Hahnl, Frank 64
Haig, Betty 42
Hall, Jim 53
Hansgen, Walt 53
Hawkes, Tom 45-47
Henrotte, George 61, 74, 77
Hill, Graham 29, 30, 38, 54, 76, 111

159